BUILDING
BRIDGE

BY

Bo Schambelan
Arnold Fisher
Richard Lederer

A FIRESIDE BOOK

A DIVISION OF SIMON & SCHUSTER

New York London Tokyo Sydney Toronto Singapore

FIRESIDE
Rockefeller Center
1230 Avenue of the Americas
New York, New York, 10020

Copyright © 1993 by Bo Schambelan, Arnold Fisher, and Richard Lederer

FIRESIDE and colophon are registered trademarks
of Simon & Schuster Inc.

Designed by Stanley S. Drate/Folio Graphics Co. Inc.
Manufactured in the United States of America

10   9   8   7   6   5   4   3   2

Library of Congress Cataloging-in-Publication Data

Fisher, Arnold.
    Building bridge / by Bo Schambelan, Arnold Fisher, and Richard
Lederer.
        p.   cm.
    "A Fireside book."
    Includes index.
    1. Contract bridge.   I. Lederer, Richard.   II. Title.
    GV1282.3.G678   1994
    795.41'5—dc20   93-25188
                                                                         CIP

ISBN: 0-671-87078-5

Contents

Introduction

Bridge is an absorbing, wonderful game that took genera-
tions to create. Evolved from whist and auction bridge, modern contract bridge is one of our great collective inventions.
It is a game for young minds of all ages. There are few more
pleasant ways to pass an evening with friends.

Bridge is elaborately designed to pleasure your mind.
You can deal a deck of cards and play Fish, but you can
also deal the same pasteboards and play what is universally
admired as the champagne of card games.

You can play bridge anywhere in the world. All you
have to learn is to count from one to seven in the new language and eight more words—the words that your host coun-
try uses for clubs, diamonds, hearts, spades, No Trump,
double, redouble, and pass. There is not a major city in the
world that does not have a bridge column in one or more of
its newspapers. More books have been written about bridge
than about any other card game.

There are enclaves of gambling where bridge is played
for high stakes, but it is also a game often played into the
wee hours without a penny bet. What accounts for its excitement and fascination? Why does the brain glow and the
heart pound when nothing rides on the play of the cards
except the game itself?

Good question. We are not really certain of the answer,
but we'll offer a few ideas here.

All of the elements of bridge are . . . well . . . so nice, so
clever a claim on your mind, so satisfying to the part of your
brain that wants to create.

About once every four hands, you get to play two hands
at once. You are on offense, as master of the battlefield, able
to see much and to map your strategy from the start. Most

hands will turn on one or two decisions, and the outcome of your planning and your campaign will be revealed almost immediately.

There is suspense. There are risks, but they are rational. It is exciting to see the pattern, to execute, and to have it work. It is not a stingy game. If you plan well, more often than not you will reap your reward. Life may not be fair, but bridge is fair.

Half the time, you will be on defense. Although you are the underdog because your opponents have been dealt the cannons, you are given the opening salvo, to attack their weakest position. The scoring is designed to tempt your opponents to bid too high. You can sabotage their plans.

Bridge is a partnership game. You communicate with your partner through the bidding. Lovers of codes delight in the tidy language of bridge bidding. When you are on defense, you can give signals, legal signals! When the special communication of bridge works, it is a thing of beauty and a joy forever.

Bridge has the thrill of luck, and luck reveals itself in every deal of the cards—mysterious, shiny beauties whose designs are centuries old. It also has much, much more than luck to it. It is an exciting tournament of minds.

Luck. Skill. Challenge. Master. Underdog. Signals. Significance snatched from swirling data, order from chaos. Temptation. Sabotage. Suspense. Risk. Codes of communication. Reason and reward. New opportunities springing eternal. A true game—and with all of that, it is refreshing and relaxing.

It is open to everyone—if you can sit upright in a chair, you can play bridge. It is one of the least expensive forms of entertainment that you can find. All you need is a table and four chairs, a deck of cards, a pad of paper, a pencil—and four people.

We wrote this book for three groups of people: beginners; people who have played bridge before, but lost touch with it and need a refresher course; and current players who feel they never mastered the fundamentals.

Most bridge players were taught to play by a hodge-podge of amateur instructors who were unsure themselves or by no instructor at all. The effect of that early training was that many of us played in a confused state. We then either gave up or played "by the seat of our pants."

Reading this book is a much better way to learn bridge than learning at the table. Even if your friends were patient, you might still be tempted to pretend to understand. Many a newcomer was first dragged to the table by three players who needed a "fourth." He or she was taught to pick up cards and follow suit like a robot. The amazing thing is that many bridge robots still were able to see that there was something special about the game.

This is not a book for advanced players. There are plenty of those. They are usually teeming with information that is not organized for the beginner. We know that pace is important; some things can be learned quickly, and some things need more time and more examples.

Bridge is a game in which you have to learn many things, all at once, in order to play at all. It takes time simply to learn the basics, and you lose out if you are not given a solid sense of the game right from the start.

This is your introduction to the world of bridge. Don't think of it as a lesson to be endured and hastily gotten through. We think that your first steps in bridge should be enjoyable in themselves. So . . . relax. Permit yourself the luxury of taking it a careful step at a time, as you build your knowledge of the game.

There are fundamentals to be learned, and this book teaches them in an organized fashion. You will find many quizzes. They are all designed to teach and to reinforce what you have already learned.

The best approach to equip you to play bridge is to explain, as clearly as we can, the logic and patterns of the game. The many examples in this book will lay a foundation on which you can build your skills. You will come to recognize familiar shapes, in many hands, and you will know what to do.

The book is designed to repeat things enough times, in one way or another, so that you will simply become conversant with the new words and ideas, and you will remember them. When it is time to "memorize," by which we mean jamming it into your brain by whatever method you choose, we will tell you and help you with it. There is a lot to learn, but there is not much to memorize.

Look at the cards, do all the quizzes, and you will learn. Don't be concerned if you get an answer wrong, as long as you go back over it and understand the reasoning. *When you finish the book, you will be more than a beginner. You will be a solid beginner.* You will be able to hold your own respectably and enjoyably in a foursome.

Let us make a great claim. Bridge will activate your love of logic, organization, and design. And while you are devoting your conscious mind to the game, your unconscious mind will start coming up with solutions to other puzzles.

When you finish reading the book, find three people and a table and a nice new deck of cards and begin. Have the newcomers read the book. Learn and enjoy together.

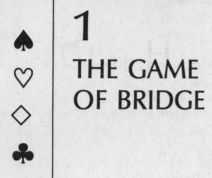

1
THE GAME
OF BRIDGE

Bridge is played by four people with a deck of fifty-two cards.

There are four suits:

Clubs	♣
Diamonds	♢
Hearts	♡
Spades	♠

The suits are ranked from low to HIGH—clubs, diamonds, hearts, spades:

Notice that the names of the suits, from lowest to HIGH-EST, are in alphabetical order.

CLUBS DIAMONDS **H**EARTS **S**PADES

Four players sit around a table.

For convenience, we call the players North, East, South, and West.

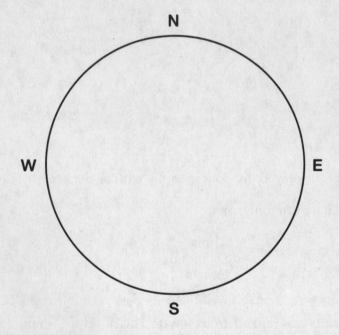

Throughout this book, North and West are male and South and East are female.

To begin, the deck is shuffled and placed in the middle of the table. Each player picks a card. High card deals. If there is a tie, then the player with the card from the highest suit wins the deal.

Question: The players pick cards:

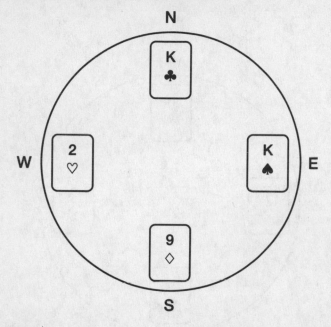

Who deals?

Just a minute. You will usually find the answer to a problem immediately following the question. Before you look at our answer, make certain that you have your answer as clear as a chime in your head.

All right. Now look back at the table and the cards. Who deals?

Answer: East. East and North both have picked a king. East has the ♠K. North has the ♣K. The ♠K is higher than the ♣K.

Once again, the suits, from HIGHEST to lowest, are:

Question: The players pick these cards. Who deals?

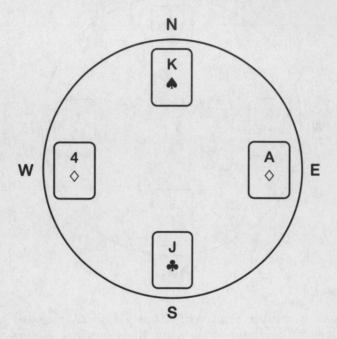

Answer: East. She picked an ace. No one else did. (If someone else had also picked an ace, then the player who picked the higher-ranking ace would be the dealer.)

Next, after the dealer is chosen, he or she deals the cards, clockwise, one at a time, until each player has thirteen cards.

Next, pick up your cards and arrange them by suits. Usually, players arrange their cards by alternating the black and the red suits, to avoid mixing up cards of the same color. Don't let anyone else see your cards. "Play them close to the vest."

Here are your cards:

Arrange them like this:

You're now ready to bid and play the hand. That is bridge!

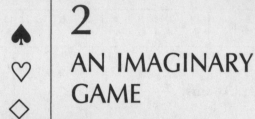

2

AN IMAGINARY GAME

Forget about bridge for a while and let us explain a similar game for four players in which you choose for deal and everyone gets thirteen cards.

In this game, the dealer leads by playing a card and everyone follows in turn, clockwise. The rule is that you have to play a card in the same suit that the leader played. Everyone "follows suit." High cards wins.

Each time four cards are played, it's called a "trick."

Question: How many tricks will complete a hand in this game?
Answer: Thirteen. There will be thirteen tricks clockwise around the table, with a winner on each trick.

The rule is that the winner of each trick leads on the next trick. In other words, he or she plays the next card—a card from the same suit that was played on the previous trick or from any other suit. The winner of the hand is the person who takes the most tricks.

That is a very simple game. Let's see if you can play it.

Question: You are North, the player at the top of the table. It is the beginning of the hand. On the first trick, West leads the ♡10.

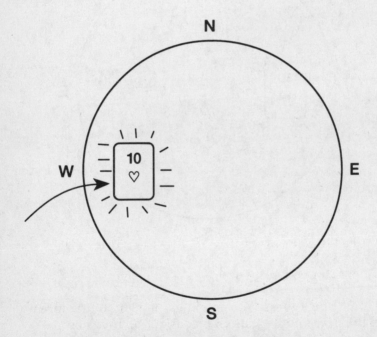

It's your turn to play. What can you play?
Answer: The ♡A or the ♡Q or the ♡8. You have to follow suit.

Question: We are well into the hand. Seven tricks have been played. It is the eighth trick. You're still sitting at the top of the table and the player to your right leads the ♣10:

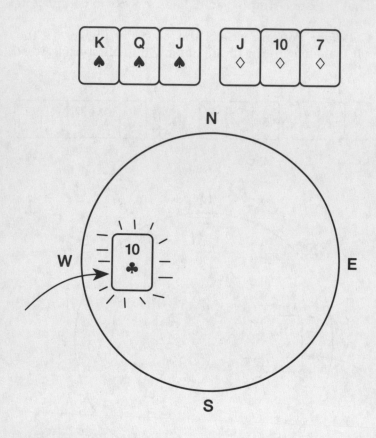

What can you play?

Wait. Don't guess. You might get it right, but you really need to know another rule. Look at our answer now.

Answer: Any card you want. That's the rule. If you cannot follow suit, you can play *any* card in your hand. (You have to play a card.) However, only the highest card in the suit led originally can win.

Let's suppose that we are still playing this imaginary game and you are dealt this hand:

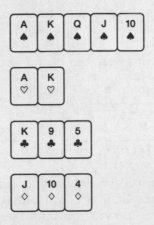

How many tricks do you think you might take? Look at the hand.

Well. There are seven cards that are going to take tricks. The ♡A, the ♡K, and the ♠A, ♠K, ♠Q, ♠J, ♠10. When you play the ♡A, no one will be able to beat it. When you play the ♡K, no one will be able to beat it. Similarly, since you hold the five highest spades, no one will be able to top you when you play one. (The next-highest spade that *either* opponent holds is the ♠9.) And the ♣K is a definite maybe—that may be an eighth trick.

Question: Do you think that you have a good hand?

Answer: Fact is, it's a beauty. You have seven winners and maybe one more. (That ♣K looks awfully good, but it isn't "sure." The ♣A might capture it.)

In a game of thirteen tricks and four players, if all of the players are playing for themselves, and if you have seven winners, you have been dealt more than your share. In fact, *four* sure winners are more than your share. In this imaginary game, with seven winners, you will win the hand.

Now let's spice up this imaginary game. We decide that
the player who wins the deal can, after looking at the cards,
designate any suit to possess "extra power."

The deal goes around. Each time you are the dealer, you
name the suit with the "extra power."

Question: If you were the dealer and you dealt yourself
this hand

which suit would you choose to have extra power?
Answer: Spades. Oh yes. You didn't even have to know
exactly what "extra power" means to answer this question.
(You definitely have the knack for this game.) Spades just
cry out to you to be the power suit. You not only have ♠K
and ♠Q, you have a boodle of them.

You don't want any other suit to be the power suit. The
other players can't have very many spades.

But we have to be clear about how the power suit exercises its power.

This is the rule: If another player plays a suit and you
are out of that suit, you can still play any card you want. If
you play a card from the power suit, your card wins over the
card in the other suit.

We call the power suit the "trump" suit. You can
"trump" ("triumph over") the other suit.

EXTRA POWER:

A deuce of trump beats an ace in any other suit.

EXTRA POWER:

The only card that can beat a trump is a higher trump.

Question: In this hand, you are North. You deal and you
name diamonds as trump. We are down to five tricks. West
leads the ♣Q. What can you play?

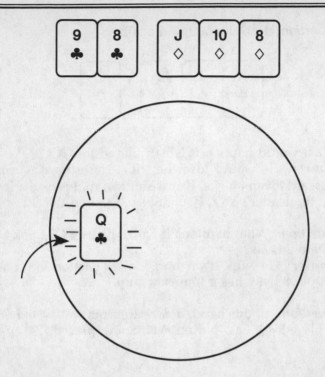

Answer: ♣9 or ♣8. You still have clubs. The rules say that you still have to follow suit. You may play any card from that suit. We jumped back a little in the lesson—to keep you on your toes.

Question: In this hand we're down to four cards. East named diamonds as trump. West leads ♡J. This is North's hand:

What card can North play?
Answer: Any card he wants to. He's out of hearts. He doesn't have to follow suit.

Question: Here is the hand again:

What would happen if North played the ♠A?

Answer: He would lose the trick. Here the ♠A would be a discard. Even an ace, if it is not trump, loses to a lower card in the leader's suit. Remember, West led the ♡J.

Question: What happens if North plays ◇Q? Look back before you answer.

Answer: He wins. It's trump. Unless East or South, who haven't played yet, has a higher trump.

Question: In this hand, hearts are trump. West led ♣10. North played ♣J. East played ♣K. South played ♡4:

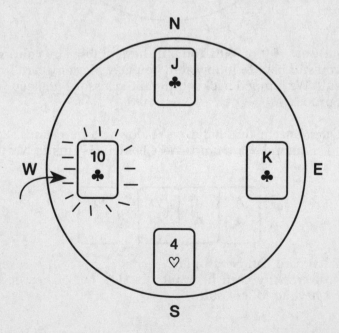

Who won the trick?

Answer: South. She played a power card. A low trump beats a higher card in a side suit.

So, in our imaginary game, after all of the cards are played, we count who has the tricks (the little piles of four cards that the winner of each trick has scooped up). The player with the most is the winner.

That is how you play that game. Trump. Side suits. Following suit if you can. Thirteen tricks. Discards. Ace is high. Nothin' to it.

Advanced question in the imaginary game: It is the twelfth trick. Hearts are trump. East leads the ♣K. You are South. As the first eleven tricks were played, you counted the trumps as they were played. Twelve trumps have been played. Only one is left in play, and that is ♡4 in your hand.

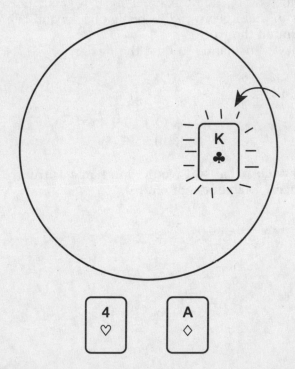

What do you play?

Answer: ♡4. By playing ♡4, you will win the trick. When you win the trick, you also win the lead. You will play the ◇A on the final trick. You have to. It's the only card you'll have. No one can beat you, because there is no higher diamond than the ace, and you know that your opponents do not have any trump.

If you played the ◇A on the twelfth trick, it would have been a discard. No matter what anyone led, you would have to win the thirteenth trick with your trump, since it would be the most powerful card left in play. However, you would have taken one trick, when you definitely could have taken two. Never good. In bridge as in life, timing is crucial.

It is very important that you follow our logic and that our explanation chimes in your brain. Remember, East led the ♣K. Hearts were trump. Don't go on until you can look back at the problem and the answer is obvious to you.

From now on, for the most part, we will portray the cards as they are portrayed in bridge books and bridge columns around the world.

Look at this hand. You are the dealer:

♠ 7
♡ K Q 3
◇ A Q J 10 9 4
♣ K 10 9

Question: What suit would you name as trump?
Answer: Diamonds, of course.

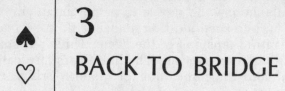

3

BACK TO BRIDGE

It's time to return to bridge—a game we never really left. The elements of the imginary game are contained in the real game of bridge.

Review: You choose for the deal. After the deal, you pick up your cards, look at them, and arrange them in order within each suit. Then you bid. Now we want to explain bidding, using vocabulary you have already learned.

New material: The players bid for the right to name trump. The dealer bids first. The bidding goes around the table clockwise until no one bids anymore.

Actually, when you bid in bridge, you bid not only for the right to name trump. You must also state the number of tricks you think you can take. As, for example, "I will attempt to take seven tricks with hearts as trump." In order to stay in the auction, you have to keep making higher bids.

You can't just recklessly call out higher bids. How high you bid depends on your evaluation of the strength of your cards. If you fail to take the number of tricks that you predict you will take, you "go down," that is, you accrue penalty points for failing to "make your bid."

That combination—the desire to name trump and the fact that you have to keep bidding higher to do so—creates one of the beautiful tensions of the game. Three players finally pass. It is like an auction. The bidding is also called "the auction," and the forerunner of modern bridge was called auction bridge.

Question: You are South and hold this hand:

♠ 7 2
♡ A K Q J 10 9 8 7
◇ A K
♣ 4

What do you think of this hand, and what would you bid?

Answer: This hand is a monster. You can barely contain yourself.

Let's look at it. It is certain that you want hearts to be trump. How many tricks do you think you can take? The ♡A through the ♡7. That's eight. The ◇AK. That's ten. If you did not know bridge vocabulary for bidding, which we haven't covered yet, you would bid, "Ten hearts." In other words, "I will take ten tricks with hearts as trump."

While you are so excited about this monstrous hand, it's a good time to get some vocabulary straight.

In bridge, the gods that watch the auction and the play have decreed that any upstart who gets to name trump must begin above the level of six tricks. They have made it a rule. Bid to make at least seven. "Six," they say, "when you get to name trump, is not much of a sportsperson's bid. After all, six is less than a majority of the tricks. Six," proclaim the gods, "is not a bid worthy of this auction. If you dare to enter the bidding, you should have at least the gumption to try for seven tricks."

These gods are snooty. Seven, they have observed, is only a bare majority of tricks. In fact, they don't even want to pay lip service to those first six tricks.

"Just say 'one' if you mean 'seven.' We know you can take the first six."

Question: So, if you want to bid to make seven tricks with diamonds as trump, what do you say?
Answer: "One diamond."

Here are more samples of this language:

"Two hearts."   "I will take eight tricks
                            with hearts as trump."

"Four clubs."   "I will take ten tricks
                            with clubs as trump."

"Seven spades."   "I will take thirteen tricks
                            with spades as trump."
                                    or
                            "I will win 'em all."

Another word to describe those first six tricks is "book." In the play, when you take your first six tricks, you have made your "book."

Review: A "seven" bid is the highest bid. A "one" bid is the lowest bid.

Question: You want to bid to take nine tricks with diamonds as trump. What do you say?
Answer: "Three diamonds."

Question: West dealt. Who bids first?
It's an easy question that you could easily slip on. Take your time. Be certain.
Answer: West. Dealer always begins the bidding.

Question: What does it mean when you bid four hearts?
Answer: "I will take ten tricks with hearts as trump."

Question: You are East and dealer. What would you bid with this hand?

> ♠ A 6 2
> ♡ A K Q J 10 9
> ◇ 5 4
> ♣ 8 2

Answer: "One heart." You have six heart tricks. You have a sure trick with the ♠A. So, if hearts are trump, you have seven tricks. Your bid accurately describes the potential of your hand to take at least "one more than six" of the tricks. In this hand, actually, you have done more than describe a potentiality. In this hand, you will definitely take seven tricks.

In addition, your partner might have a few winners.

Your partner?

In bridge, you have a partner, and he or she sits across the table from you.

North and South are partners.

East and West are partners.

You win and lose with your partner.

You share the ups and downs.

Even-Steven.

No excuses.

You are in it together.

Partnership is one of the greatest challenges in the bidding and play of the hand. It involves the necessity for communication. It is what makes bridge great.

Up to this point, when we have asked you to analyze the trick-taking power of a hand, we have assumed that you were in it by yourself. We have asked you to evaluate your hand while looking only at the tricks that you could take by yourself. In the actual game, however, your partner's hand, hopefully, will complement yours. Your bids will give information about your hand, but you will not be describing how many tricks you can take on your own. You will be describing your hand in an effort to explore with your partner the number of tricks you can take together. This is bridge. And one obvious corollary of what we have just said is that you need not, by your opening bid, assure your partner that you have seven sure tricks in your hand, in order to enter the auction.

Modern bridge is also called "contract bridge," because the last bidder in the auction "wins the contract"—that is, agrees to play to make the bid. But you will do so with the combined strength of the partnership. In fact, your partner joins in the agreement by passing out of the auction.

It is possible, therefore, that you might bid "one spade" with only three sure tricks, everyone else passes, you play the hand, your partner has no high cards at all (and had no choice but to pass), and you get creamed. But this is very unlikely. If you and your partner don't have the power, the opponents will, and they will enter the auction and take you out of your potentially unmakable "one spade" bid. Very few bridge hands get passed out at the one level. The bidding must be seen, especially at that level, as, first and foremost, a legal means to communicate through agreed-upon codes.

"One spade" was meant to tell your partner about your hand. It wasn't a guarantee that you could take seven tricks. Every once in a while, it won't work out. That is life. That is bridge. At least, in bridge, that sort of disaster is rare.

In bridge, a partnership consists of two people who play East-West or North-South and who have very specific understandings with each other about how they will bid and play. After the cards are dealt, they communicate only by their bids and by the play of their cards.

Review: The bidding goes around the table. The dealer bids first.

New material: Many times when it is your turn to bid, you look at your cards and decide that you had better stay out of the auction. That decision is, very often, the very best one you can make. You say, "Pass." "Pass" is a bid.

There are two other bids that you must know about—
"double" and "redouble."

At any point in the bidding, after your opponent has
bid, you can "double." That is a bid. Technically, your bid
doubles the stakes. It is a wager that your opponent will not
be able to make the bid, that he or she will "go down."

(Actually, "double" often acts as a code to tell your partner something specific about your hand. More about that
later.)

After you double, if an opponent thinks that their partnership really can make the bid, he or she can raise the
stakes even further by saying "redouble." That is a bid. It,
also, can act as a code.

Once the cards are dealt, your bids are the only language
that you may use to describe your hand to your partner. You
are permitted to use bids that are really "artificial" codes.
(For example, "one club" can mean "I've been dealt a
beauty.") And, in the play, the order in which you select to
play your cards can be used as "signals."

However, the tapping of feet under the table and the
subtle placements of your fingers on your cards are viola-
tions not only of the letter but the spirit of the Rules. They
don't even debate it anymore.

Question: May you decide with your partner that if you
bid in a high voice, you have a so-so hand, and if you bid in
a low voice you have a whopper?

Answer: Yes. In Samarkand, with a scimitar. Anywhere
else, no way.

Question: What does "going down" mean?

Answer: The person who won the auction makes fewer
tricks than he or she contracted to take.

If the player does make the number of tricks contracted,
then he or she has "made the hand."

Not infrequently, you will be dealt a hand that looks like this:

> ♠ K Q 7 6
> ♡ A J 3
> ◇ K 7 2
> ♣ Q J 10

What do you notice? Every suit has just about the same number of cards as every other suit. It is a very nice hand, but it is difficult to choose a trump suit. You might be tempted to play the hand without naming a power suit. With this hand, we would bid, "One No Trump." That bid describes the hand. In a No-Trump contract, there is no power suit. High card wins.

Review: The dealer begins the bidding, and it goes around clockwise.

Review: The suits are ranked in order:

Now we can add a bid:

You must bid up the ladder.

If the player before you (your "right-hand opponent," or "righty") bids 2♡, you can't bid 1♠.

If "righty" bids 2♡, you can't bid 2◇.

If "righty" bids 2♡, you can bid 2♠, or anything higher. You can, for example, jump to 3NT.

Question: Other than "pass," what is the lowest bid in bridge? What is the highest?

Answer: The lowest is 1♣; the highest is 7NT ("I will take thirteen tricks and there is no trump suit").

Review: After a bid, if three people in a row pass, the bidding is over. The last bid before the three passes, which is also the highest bid, is the "contract."

The partnership that bid the contract "plays the hand."

The other partnership "defends." They try to defeat the contract.

Look at the bidding. North is the dealer:

N	E	S	W
P	1♣	Double	1♠
2♡	Pass	Pass	Pass

The bidding is completed. The contract is 2♡. East-West will defend. North is the "declarer." That means that he is on the team that won the auction and he was the first member of that team to name—to "declare"—the contract suit. In this hand, he was the only member of the team to name the contract suit.

South's "double" was only a double of East's bid of 1♣. It was wiped out as soon as West bid 1♠.

Question: In this hand, the bidding was:

N	E	S	W
1♠	Pass	2◇	Pass
3◇	Pass	4♠	Pass
Pass	Pass		

Who is the declarer?

Answer: North. His team won the auction. They will play the hand. North is the member of the North-South team that first bid spades. Even though his partner made the final bid of 4♠, North was the player that declared them.

Question: West is the dealer.
The bidding:

N	E	S	W
			Pass
1♣	Pass	?	

Can South bid 2♡?

Answer: Yes. It is up the ladder. In fact, it is a jump up the ladder. She can bid just 1♡. But she may want to bid 2♡! She seems to be trying to say something.

Here is her hand. Look it over:

> ♠ 7 4
> ♡ A K J 10 7 6
> ◇ A Q 10
> ♣ K J

It's a monster, and her partner, North, opened the bidding. They are going places.

Here are both hands:

North
> ♠ A Q 8 2
> ♡ Q 3
> ◇ 6 3 2
> ♣ A Q 10 7

South
> ♠ 7 4
> ♡ A K J 10 7 6
> ◇ A Q 10
> ♣ K J

How about that? They have more tricks than decent folks should have.

After the bidding is completed, the defender to the left of the declarer plays the first card. He or she takes the card—any card—from his or her hand and puts it in the middle of the table. This is called the "opening lead." After that, the play proceeds clockwise.

There is one more fundamental thing to learn about the game of bridge. This may be the favorite among the many rules that make bridge so special.

After the opening lead, it is the declarer's partner's turn to play a card. Amazingly, he lays down all of his cards, face up at his place at the table, for anyone to see, nicely arranged by suits and in order. The declarer's partner does this in every hand. For the rest of the hand, he sits without disturbing anyone. He makes no decisions in the play. He is the "dummy." His hand is called the "dummy." In every hand, there is a "dummy." The play is up to dummy's partner, the declarer. Declarer will play a card from dummy.

Review: After the opening lead, the dummy is laid down. The dummy is arranged on the table like this:

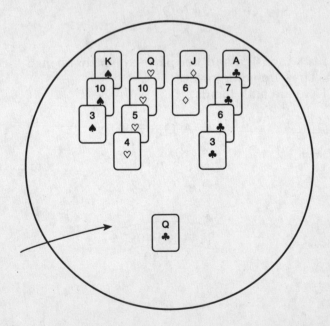

The declarer plays a card from dummy. The other defender then plays a card. Declarer then plays a card from her hand. That is trick one.

Declarer will play the cards in the dummy, as well as the cards in her own hand. When it is dummy's turn to play, declarer can call for the card to be played from dummy, and her partner, in strict obedience, and even if he thinks it is a terrible play, will quietly lift the called-for card and place it in the middle of the table. Or, as is often done, declarer can reach across the table and play the dummy's card herself.

Review: After declarer plays a card from dummy, the declarer's right-hand opponent ("righty") plays. Then the declarer plays a card from her hand. Four cards to a trick.

Declarer will play each card, from dummy, and from her hand, in its turn, but she will never lose sight of the fact that dummy's hand and her hand are cooperating members of the same team.

In this hand, North-South won the contract. South is the declarer. West, at the left of the declarer, leads ♣Q:

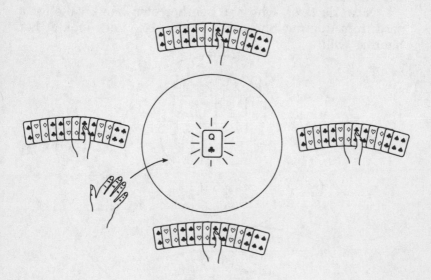

The dummy lays down his hand:

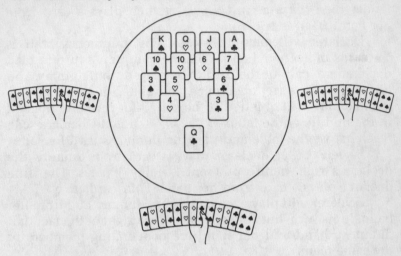

All of the players can see the dummy. The defenders can't see each other's hands. The declarer can't see the defenders' hands. So, everybody gets to see two hands—his or her own, and the dummy's.

Next, declarer, who can see her own hand, calls for a card from dummy. She calls for the ♣A. Let's look at her hand as well:

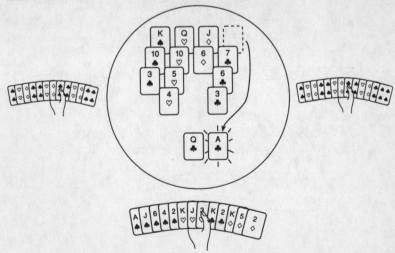

Question: Why did declarer play the ♣A?
Answer: To win the trick.

After declarer played the ♣A, East followed suit with the ♣4:

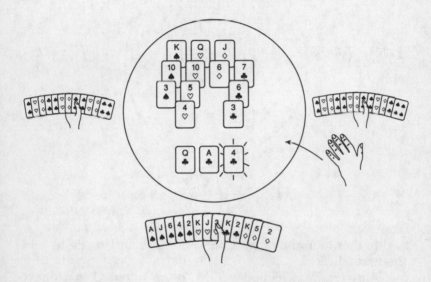

Question: What should declarer play from her hand?
Answer: The ♣2. She could play the ♣K, but it would be wasted. Playing it under the ♣A would be the same as discarding it. Now, she can hold her ♣K for another trick.
The trick is complete.

Question: Besides the ♣K, what is the highest club still in play? See if you can get the answer without looking at the cards. Then go back and look at the diagram.
Answer: The ♣J. Either East or West has it.

Question: Let's go back to the opening lead. Here is the hand again:

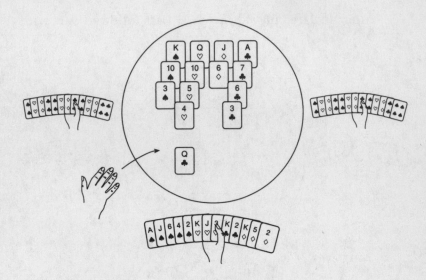

Is there another play that declarer could make to win the first trick?

Answer: Yes. Declarer could "duck" the ♣Q in dummy and, instead of playing the ♣A, she could play the ♣3. East follows suit. Now, when declarer plays from her hand, she could play the ♣K rather than the ♣2 and still win the trick.

4

KEEPING SCORE

Scoring is vital in bridge, and it must be kept in mind both when you bid and when you play. There are bonuses for bidding and making certain levels of contracts. That is, if you bid and make these contracts, the score doesn't always just go up step-by-step, but can leap in value. Therefore, sometimes it makes sense to stretch the values in your hand—to take the risk and bid for a tougher, higher contract—because that bid will take you to a new scoring plateau.

At other times, when it looks as if the other team has the cards and is going to win the bid, it makes sense, in what is really a defensive position, to stretch your bid and to sacrifice, because the penalty for going down may be less than the points that the other team could score if they won the auction. Sometimes, it makes sense to use your bid to force the other team to try for a higher contract than they wanted to settle for, and to keep them out of an easy score.

In other words, it may be better to bid and play 5♢ and

go down (as you will see later, when we get more specific, the other team would score 50 points) than to let the other team play the contract at 4♡ (the other team could score 120 points). Of course, you had better make a good assessment of how many tricks you might go down, because losing too many tricks can be very costly.

Sometimes, apart from concerns about scoring, you interject a bid in order to gum up the other side's communication.

Bridge is not about achieving a preset goal. You do not set out to perform one task, such as capture the opponent's king, as in chess. In bridge, you play for the optimum result. Bridge is a game where, in every hand, you play to win with the cards that you are dealt. You do the best that you can with those cards. If your team wasn't dealt the power on this hand, you can be sure that the other team was. The scoring system influences them to bid as high as they can, in order to achieve a maximum score.

If they bid to take twelve tricks, they can afford to lose only one trick. You will need only two tricks to defeat them. Your lonely king and jack will start to look very interesting. The clash in bridge occurs at the point to which the other team is stretched. You will let them have eleven tricks. They will let you have one trick. All during the rounds of play, the battle will be for that one swing trick.

Many, many hands in bridge are like that. The game is beautifully designed—to be close on almost every hand.

We will give you all of the rules of scoring later. You don't need to know all of the specifics now, just a few important things.

As the bridge gods have proclaimed, you as declarer get no points for your first six tricks. After those, you get 20, 30, or 40 points per trick, depending on your trump suit.

Clubs and diamonds score the least. They are called the "minor suits." Hearts and spades are a second, higher, scoring category. They are called the "major suits." No Trump is the highest.

Contract Suit	Scoring Points per Trick (Over Six)
NT	40 for the first trick,
	30 for each additional trick
♠	30
♡	30
◇	20
♣	20

The scoring, as you can see, favors No Trump, hearts, and spades. This has an important effect on your strategy during the auction.

Take a look at the chart. If you bid and make 5♣, you score 100 points. That's hardly a bountiful score for taking eleven tricks.

If you bid and make 3NT, you score 100 points. Nine tricks. It looks like a bargain.

If you bid and make 4♠, you score 120 points.

Question: How many points do you score if you bid and make 3◇?

Answer: 60.

You create the chance for bonuses by bidding and making contracts that give you a score of 100 points or more. 100 points is "game":

3NT = game (100 points)
4 ♡ = game (120 points)
4 ♠ = game (120 points)
5 ♣ = game (100 points)
5 ◇ = game (100 points)

These five contracts are the "game" contracts. Making "game" contracts creates the chance for bonuses.

We realize that you want to know what the bonuses are. A bridge contest is called a "rubber." These are the bonuses. When one team scores two "games," the "rubber" is over. That is the end of the contest. You get a bonus of 500 points if you win two out of three games. You get an even larger bonus, 700 points, if you win two games in a row.

As defenders, you get 50 points for each undertrick—

that is, each trick your opponents overbid. After a team makes a game, the risks get higher for them—each undertrick is worth 100 points to the opponents. (It is possible for you to accumulate so many defensive points that even though your opponents score two "games," and get bonus points, you will end up with more total points and win the rubber.)

Review: The five game-level bids are 3NT, 4♡, 4♠, 5♣, and 5◇.

You also get bonus points for bidding and making contracts at the levels of 12 or 13 tricks. These are called "slams":

> 12 tricks = small slam
> 13 tricks = grand slam

Slams are worth lots of bonus points. It takes considerable power to make a slam. You need good cards.

If you think that your opponent has bid too high, you can "double." It is a bid that says, "I bet you won't make it," and it raises the stakes. Your opponent, if really confident, can raise the stakes even further by bidding, "redouble," which says, "Oh yes I will."

Trying to bid and make "game" contracts is the essence of bridge. You and your partner are always exploring the possibility of "game" through your bids.

Question: What are the game contracts?

Answer: 3NT, 4♡, 4♠, 5♣, 5◇. It's really important that you know these intimately.

Notice that if you bid a game in No Trump, you need to take only nine tricks.

If you bid a game in hearts or spades, you must take ten tricks.

And if you bid a game in clubs or diamonds, you must take eleven tricks.

Playing without a trump suit, in 3NT, can be tricky. Trying to take ten tricks in 4♡ or 4♠ is easier than taking eleven tricks in 5♣ or 5◇. No wonder that bidders struggle to find fits with their partners in hearts or spades.

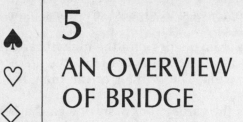

5
AN OVERVIEW
OF BRIDGE

You have now learned the basics of the game.

Really, at this point, you could deal 'em and play. You have absorbed a lot. You might be timid at first, but you would soon see that a game with three other people who had no more background than you would quickly develop into an interesting evening. But we recommend that you read on.

Rather than testing you with many problems at this point, we want to give you a summary of the rules of the game of bridge. This summary should now make a great deal of sense to you, and you should understand it easily. Don't be concerned with memorizing. But read it carefully. It is an important part of the lesson. If everything clicks, you are doing just fine. If there is something that you want to review at any time, just flip back through the previous chapters. We have supplied you with an index, to make this easy for you.

• The game is played with a fifty-two-card deck and two teams of two players.

- There are four suits in the deck with thirteen cards in each suit, each suit ranging from 2 to ace. Ace is high. The suits, in order from lowest to highest, are clubs, diamonds, hearts, and spades.
- The players draw from the deck for the highest card. If two or more players draw cards of equal rank, the player with the highest suit wins. The winner of the draw becomes the dealer.
- The dealer deals the cards clockwise, one card at a time, giving the first card to the player at his left, until all cards are dealt.
- When the players have had the opportunity to arrange their cards and to study them for a reasonable period of time, the dealer bids first. Dealer may bid any suit, or No Trump, and may bid as low as "1♣" (he or she bids to take seven tricks with clubs as trump), or as high as "7NT." (He or she bids to take thirteen tricks without a trump suit.) Dealer may also "pass."
- The bid goes around clockwise. Each successive player may bid, as long as the bid is higher than the previous bid.
- All bidders may also pass or double or redouble.
- When three players have passed consecutively, the auction is closed. The auction is won by the partnership that has offered the highest bid. They have contracted to make their bid.
- If the contract is in a suit, rather than No Trump, then that suit is called "trump."
- The member of the partnership who first bid the contract suit is called the declarer.
- The declarer's partner is called the dummy.
- The opposing team are called the defenders.
- The first card played is called the opening lead, and it is led by the declarer's left-hand opponent—"lefty." He is well advised to give his opening lead some thought. He wants to take a trick, to help his partner to take a trick, or to play a card that will promote a trick somewhere down the line.
- The dummy is laid down.

- The declarer plays a card from the dummy. The next player plays a card, and the declarer follows from her hand.
- When each hand has played a card—four cards in all— that is called a "trick."
- The declarer calls the dummy's plays. The dummy obeys and plays the requested card, or the declarer just reaches across the table and plays the card.
- On each trick, each player must follow suit with any card in that suit.
- A player who is void in a suit may play any card in his or her hand. He or she may play a trump card or discard. The decision is entirely tactical.
- Any card in the trump suit beats any other card except a higher trump. In a No-Trump contract, the ace of the suit that is led is always high.
- The hand that wins the trick leads the first card of the next trick. If the trick was won by a card from dummy, then the declarer will lead a card from dummy.
- The hand is completed when thirteen tricks have been played.
- If the contract is achieved, the hand is made.
- If the contract is not achieved, the hand is down.
- The scoring is in accordance with the rules of rubber bridge (See Chapters 4 and 22).
- The deal goes clockwise for the rest of the hands.

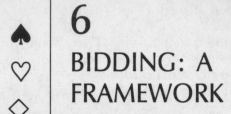

6
BIDDING: A FRAMEWORK

Bidding is the language of bridge. It is the only way that you have to describe to your partner what your hand looks like. It is a legal means of communication. Many times, you can choose among many bids. If the only bid so far is 1♡ and it is your turn, you are permitted by the rule to bid anything from 1♠ to 7NT, since they would all be higher bids.

But you are not seeking simply to spin the wheel. You want to communicate with your partner as accurately as you can. You want to choose the right bid, and this chapter will explain how.

The purpose of every bid is to describe your hand.

When you deal a deck of cards, the number of possible card combinations is astronomical. But, there are only fifteen "words" that you may use in the language of bidding communication.

"One" "two" "three" "four" "five" "six" "seven" = 7
"Clubs" "diamonds" "hearts" "spades"
"No Trump"   = 5
"Pass"   = 1
"Double" "Redouble"   = <u>2</u>
      TOTAL   15

In fact, these words combine to make only thirty-eight possible bids:

Four possible suit bids at each of seven levels
  (1♣, 1◇, 1♡, 1♠, 2♣, 2◇, 2♡, etc.)   = 28
One possible NT bid at each of seven levels   = 7
"Pass," "double," and "redouble"   = <u>3</u>
      TOTAL   38

The 15 "words" are the only "words" that you may use in the language of bidding communication. That language has a limited vocabulary. We have 15 "words" that combine into 38 "phrases" to describe 635,013,559,600 different hands.

That is what's fun about bridge. You can make it work. You can make the bids into a code that speaks about your hand. It could be very simple; "1♡" could mean "I have hearts."

You and your partner are always casting out your bids in the effort to find a "fit," two hands that will play well together. You are primarily looking for a trump fit. You can't see your partner's hand. In bridge, the search for a "fit" with your partner's hidden hand is the heart of your bidding. In a way, it is as if 1♡ might say, "How about hearts?" and your partner's 2◇ bid might reply, "I don't think so, but how about diamonds?"

Question: Imagine being declarer at South with North as dummy:

North	♠ A 10
	♡ Q 10 9 8
	◇ A Q 6
	♣ J 7 4 3

South	♠ K 6
	♡ A J 7 3 2
	◇ K J 7 5
	♣ Q 10

Is this a fit? What should you have bid for trump?

Answer: It surely is. Hearts must be trump. The hands will play well together. That almost solid nine-card heart suit will put the declarer in control. Any decent bidding system should lead you to a heart contract.

Question: Look at these hands:

North	♠ A J 7 5
	♡ A 10 3 2
	◇ ———
	♣ K J 7 4 2

South	♠ K Q 10 8 2
	♡ 7 6 5
	◇ Q 10 8
	♣ A 9

Is this a fit?

Answer: Yes. North and South have that great spade trump suit between them. And do you notice that North is void in diamonds? South has weak diamonds. There is a good chance that the defenders will lead a diamond. But the defenders will get no diamond trick, because declarer will straightaway use one of dummy's spades to trump the diamond lead, and on the same trick she will toss one of her worthless diamonds from her hand. We call that a "fit"!

Codes. We are not yet teaching you a specific bidding system and its codes. We are giving you an understanding of bidding and its challenges. With this understanding, any bidding system will make sense. The specifics should be easy.

As long as you disclose your code to your opponents, you can use any system you want. For example, you could use a code in which "1♣" means "I have eleven spades, and the other two cards are no higher than a ten." That would be a very descriptive and specific code. It would be as if your partner had a window on your hand. But it is a terribly inefficient code, obviously. You will be dealt that specific hand about once every sixty-seven years. (And, boy, are you ready for it!) But if you use up your bids—the thirty-eight possible bids of your "language"—to describe very specific hands, you won't have enough bids for all the zillions of hands that don't fit the code. You won't have enough room to say all the things that you want to about all of your many hands.

The meaning that you give to your bids must be sufficiently general that you don't use them up too fast and sufficiently specific to be useful. Bridge players search for the bidding system that gives them the happiest medium, and no one has found one that is perfect. More often than not, approximation is the best you can do in bidding. Your hand may be one that falls into a gap where none of even the best available bids of your system is quite accurate—none of the "words" that you could reasonably choose at a certain point in the bidding says exactly what you would like to say. This is bridge. This is very common. You must choose the bid that best describes your hand. That is where you use your creativity and your instincts.

Here is a common story from the bridge table. Your part-

ner opens with 1♡. The next player bids 1♠. You look at
your cards:

♠ K 6 4
♡ 8 5
◇ 10 7 4
♣ A J 9 7 6

"It certainly doesn't look as if I can support the notion
of hearts as our trump suit. Oh my goodness. I would have
to bid to a higher level to tell her about these clubs. I would
have to say, '2♣.' But I don't think I have any business bidding so high with this hand. But I do have some tricks. I
can't pass. And . . . I'm not the opening bidder. So, if I bid,
I wouldn't be saying that I have the strength for an opening
bid. Maybe I could try 1NT? That's hardly a daring bid. It's
at the one level. But if bid 1NT, she will think that I have an
evenly balanced hand. What should I do?"

That little saga describes one of the most common binds
that arise at a bridge table. Never fear. In that situation, the
best bid will be pretty clear to you once you have read the
rest of this book. You will see that your partner's hand might
have only the minimum strength that your system permits
to open with the words "1♡." You cannot bid "2♣," even
though the bid is very accurate as to your best suit, because
that bid would commit the partnership to an eight-trick contract. (Your cards are not strong enough to do that. The bid
would be inaccurate as to the power in your hand.) But if
you passed, your partner would surely undervalue the
strength that you do have. Of the alternatives, "1NT" best
describes your hand. It isn't perfect. In a perfect world,
"1NT" would be misleading. But if we remember how limited our language is, it is the best bid available. In fact, if
everybody knows the limits of the language, no one is
really misled.

Let's try to think up a system. We'll refine this system
quite a bit, but for now let's suppose we decide that "1♠"
by the opening bidder means "I have five or more spades

and at least three sure tricks." By the same token, "1♡" by the opening bidder would mean that "I have five or more hearts and at least three sure tricks." If you bid "1♠," your partner won't know if you have five or six or seven or even more spades. But she surely has something to go on. Your bid has very much narrowed things down.

Actually, she has a lot to go on. She may not know the value of every spot card in your hand, but she has been told the essence of your hand. She has seen hands like that. She knows that hands like that will tend to take so many tricks. What is the essence of your hand? It is your trick-taking power and your best suit, within a certain range.

And, almost always, you will get to bid more than once. Your code can work in sequence. Your first bid can say, "I've got either this or that." Your next bid will tell which of the two it is. Bidding like that is like playing "Twenty Questions." Your first bid narrows things down, and each higher bid narrows them further. You would save a code like that for hands where you are sure that you could make a contract at a high level, since that code could take you up high very quickly. (Actually, every additional bid in every hand further clarifies the bidder's hand.)

You may guess that no matter what bidding system you use, there will be many occasions when there is no bid available to describe your hand in a "natural" way. Sometimes, you have to say "No Trump" when you would like to say "clubs." But in the world of bridge, the No-Trump bid is not really artificial. It is squeezed very naturally from the alternatives available to you.

Every bidding system sometimes uses bids that are "artificial." That is fine. But every bidding system had better find a way to keep a sharp eye out for bridge reality. Your system can't take you beyond a contract that you would really wish to play. Somehow, if your cards say that you should be playing 4♡, your system had better guide you to that as your last bid.

Any system will do. It should be a rational and, ultimately, accurate way to describe your hands to your partner. Once you and your partner know your system, and the kernel of meaning in any bid, then your bids will make more sense. They will be descriptive. All systems will have ambiguities. That is the challenge. A good bid is nothing more or less than the best bid possible.

Let's look at a hand and assume that you have not talked to your partner first. You want your bids to be as rational and descriptive as they can be. Think about your partner. Really, you are thinking about how your own mind works, and you are assuming that if both of you continue to make a constant effort to be rational, you will come to respect and to trust each other's thought processes. You have every right to assume that you two are, at least in this game, in sync. Your partner knows that you are about to attempt to describe thirteen cards, unknown to her, with one brief utterance, chosen from the thirty-eight possible.

Question: You deal yourself this hand:

♠ A K J 10 8
♡ K J 6
◇ Q 10
♣ 9 8 6

What would you bid?
Answer: 1♠.

Question: Do you think you and your partner can make 4♠?
Answer: You have no idea. You haven't heard from your partner.

But of course, you will not, in fact, leave your bidding solely up to each other's logical ability. Before the cards are taken from the box, you will communicate with your partner in ordinary language. You will agree on the system and codes you are using and discuss any fine points. Then your bids will have much greater meaning to each other when you are holding your cards.

Every bidding system must strive for the identical thing: a fit in the play—that is, two hands that work well together and consequently take lots of tricks. In this book, we have adopted the most commonly used and widely accepted bidding system in bridge. You can use it anywhere in the world. It works. The system is simple and rational, and it is used by most experts. More often than not, it will get you to the right contract, and it will keep you out of the wrong contract. When you and your partner are holding strong cards, the system is a powerful tool to get you to game contracts, particularly 4♡ and 4♠.

7

BIDDING: MORE ANALYSIS

Your partner and you are looking for fits. You are particularly looking for fits in the trump suit—specifically, a fit of eight cards or more.

If you have five trumps and your partner has three, that's a fit.

If you have four trumps and your partner has four, that's a fit. It will play even better than a five–three fit.

If you have six trumps and your partner has two, that's a fit.

Seven–one and eight–zero are not exactly "fits," since the power is in one hand, but they are great for playing.

Eight-card trump fits are the cornerstone of winning bridge: Eight or more—yes! Seven or fewer—no!

Trust the teachers. Playing with seven trumps is no fun. The hand can get out of control. Your opponents will have six trumps, and that is just giving them too much to work with. But with eight, the seesaw tilts your way. You are in control.

Look at these hands. South is declarer at 4♠.

North	♠ Q 10 8
(dummy)	♡ A K Q 8
	◇ 10 7 2
	♣ 10 9 8

South	♠ A K 9 7 6
(declarer)	♡ J 10 7
	◇ 9 4
	♣ A Q J

It is pretty obvious that declarer's weakness is in the diamond suit. It is also obvious that the defenders hold the
high diamonds, and will probably lead them. However, they
will only get two diamond winners, because on the third
diamond lead, declarer will be out of diamonds. He will
trump, and win the trick. Now he will be in control of the
hand. Now, he will decide which card to lead, and he will
put into motion his strategy for the play of the hand.

This is only one of many hands that you will see in this
book. It illustrates the power of trump. Trust us, for now,
and observe in this and in other hands, that with eight or
more trumps between you and your partner, the defenders
will not have an easy time thwarting your strategy. But with
fewer than eight trumps, things will most often not go well
for you. The defenders will simply hold too many cards of
the power suit.

Question: Declarer and dummy bid to 4♠. The opening lead is the ♡K:

North

♠ K J 9 6
♡ 7 5
◇ A K 7
♣ Q 9 3 2

"♡K"

South

♠ A Q 3 2
♡ A 10 8
◇ 6 5
♣ A 10 7 5

Is it a trump fit? How many tricks do declarer and dummy have to take to make the contract?

Answer: They need ten tricks. They have a beautiful trump fit to help them make their contract.

Let's look closer at what it means to have a "fit" by talking about the play of one bridge hand.

PLAYING A HAND

North and South bid to 4♡. West's opening lead was the ◇A. The dummy was spread on the table:

North
(dummy)

♠ K 4 3
♡ 7 6 5 3
◇ 9 5 2
♣ A 7 5

"◇A"

South (hand held
close to the vest)

♠ A 9 6
♡ A K Q J 4
◇ Q 10
♣ K Q 4

This is a very important time in the play of the hand. Now, while the opening lead and dummy sit on the table, is when you, the declarer, must pause, analyze the cards carefully, and develop the strategy for the play of the entire hand.

The basic question that you should be asking yourself is: "Where are those tricks that I contracted for going to come from? We are in four hearts. Where are those ten tricks going to come from?"

Take your time. Check every word we say:

Count, in your mind, one at a time, in both declarer's and dummy's hands, the cards that have the power to take tricks. This is called "counting your winners."

The ♠AK. That's two. The ♣AKQ. That's three more.

Hearts are trump. You hold ♡AKQJ. That's four more winners.

How many is that? Yes, nine. Make certain that all of this is clear to you before you read on. Check *everything* we say against the hand.

We think that this part of the book is so important that, before we worry about that tenth trick, we want you to take the time to get an even clearer picture about the nine tricks that we are counting on.

We are spending a great deal of time on this hand—more than we will with almost any other hand in the book—because once you know how to pay attention to the cards, the book will start talking to you like an old friend.

Remember that on every trick declarer and dummy both play a card. (So do both defenders.) After the lead, before playing any card, you should *visualize* one card played from dummy and one card played from declarer's hand. These two cards will make up one "trick," for the purpose of this exercise. So for each "trick," watch the way that the hands will cooperate by playing two cards—one from dummy's hand and one from declarer's hand—at the same time. It would not hurt to visualize the two cards coming up, together, from the two hands.

One thing is certain. Declarer will lose the first trick. West has already played ◇A for a defensive winner right off the bat with the opening lead. (See the following page.)

	♠ K 4 3
North	♡ 7 6 5 3
(dummy)	◇ 9 5 2
	♣ A 7 5

"◇A"

	♠ A 9 6
South	♡ A K Q J 4
(declarer)	◇ Q 10
	♣ K Q 4

Declarer will play ◇2 from dummy and the ◇10 from her hand.

The ◇2 and the ◇10 will be the declarer's first (losing) "trick."

West still has the lead on trick two. He plunks down the ◇K. The ◇5 from dummy and the ◇Q from declarer will be the declarer's second (losing) trick.

West's third lead is ♣J. Here are the dummy and declarer hands at trick three, just after the lead of ♣J:

	♠ K 4 3
North	♡ 7 6 5 3
(dummy)	◇ 9
	♣ A 7 5

"♣J"

	♠ A 9 6
South	♡ A K Q J 4
(declarer)	◇
	♣ K Q 4

Imagine that you decide to play ♣A from dummy and ♣4 when you get to your hand. Watch the ♣A and ♣4. They disappear from the play, and come together, faces down, next to you. It is the third trick. It is the first trick you have won.

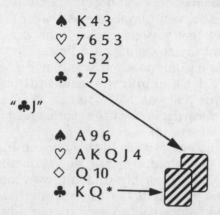

♠ K 4 3
♡ 7 6 5 3
◇ 9 5 2
♣ * 7 5

"♣J"

♠ A 9 6
♡ A K Q J 4
◇ Q 10
♣ K Q *

Now declarer will be in control.

The nine winners that you counted were ♡AKQJ, ♠AK, and ♣AKQ.

"Where is declarer?" That is a bridge player's way of asking which hand won the last trick. Dummy did—with ♣A. Declarer must play the next card from dummy's hand. You are "in dummy." Let's imagine that you will play the ♡3 from dummy and, in your turn, the ♡A from your hand.

Play the winning tricks, in pairs, in your mind, or make a tally by writing:

WINNERS:	Declarer—Dummy
	♣4 —♣A
	♡A —♡3

Here are the other winners, in pairs:

Declarer—Dummy
♡K —♡5
♡Q —♡6
♡J —♡7
♠A —♠3
♠6 —♠K
♣K —♣5
♣Q —♣7

Nine winners so far!

These are not the only combinations of cards that you could use to take these winners. For example, it would make no difference if you played the ♠4 with the ♠A. But it is crucial, now, that you clearly see nine winning tricks (and you must not use the same card twice).

You can use any method you like to keep track of your winners. We don't mind if you make little marks in the book over the cards that you have "used up." You might want to get a deck of cards, lay out the hand, and pick up the winners, two by two.

Do not go any farther in this book until you have completed this important exercise, by any method you choose. It's not that it's so terribly difficult; we simply wish to emphasize how vital it is, as the opening lead and dummy are unveiled before you, to see, in your mind, the way that dummy's and declarer's hands will cooperate.

When and where is that "tenth trick" going to come from?

Let's look more closely at the trump suit. You have nine hearts:

Dummy   ♡ 7 6 5 3

Declarer   ♡ A K Q J 4

The defenders started with only four hearts. There are a number of ways that those four hearts could be distributed in the defenders' hands. Here are some of the likely ways that they could "split":

West	East
10 9 8	2
9	10 8 2
10 2	9 8
8 2	10 9

East and West will be forced to give up all of their trumps, one at a time, in following suit to three rounds of trumps. That is, their trumps will fall on the ♡AKQ. Not only your remaining ♡J, but your fifth trump—that little heart, ♡4—will eventually be a winner.

Even if they split something like this:

West	East
10 9 8 2	—

West will still be forced to give up all of his trumps, one at a time, in four rounds of hearts. The trumps will be "drawn" from his hand. After those four rounds, you will still be left with the ♡4 for your tenth winner, on which you will discard from dummy:

$$♡4-◇9$$

or

$$♡4-♠4$$

This partnership has surely found a fit. The dummy's and declarer's hands will play beautifully together.

Now go back once more to the full hands on page 56. Don't look at our list of tricks. Add up ten winning tricks in your mind. Don't confuse the cards. Don't "play" a card more than once. Make sure that you have counted ten winners. (Using your fingers for counting is definitely permitted.) Work at this exercise for as long as you must until you are certain. Reread our explanations until they make perfect sense.

Got 'em all? Got all ten?

Good.

Now you can absolutely relax. You have played a bridge hand in your mind. That is just what bridge players do. You have crossed over—you are now a bridge player.

8

BIDDING—A CLOSER LOOK AT THE CARDS

Let's go back to the last hand we were working with in chapter 7—4♡ bid and made. We will concentrate on the bidding stage. We now know that the partnership found a beautiful fit, so let's see how they might have done it. Let's look at it from the point of view of the person who we now know will turn out to be the declarer.

East was the dealer, and she passed. You are South. Here's your hand again. At this point, these are the only cards that you can see:

♠ A 9 6
♡ A K Q J 4
♢ Q 10
♣ K Q 4

What bid most clearly describes your hand? 1♡, of course. Just one look tells you that you have been dealt a strong hand, that you definitely have the right to be in the auction, and that hearts is your best suit. That is exactly what you want to tell your partner.

West passes.

Your partner, North, bids 2♡.

What is he trying to say about his hand? It sure sounds as if you've found a trump fit. It sure sounds as if he's trying to be encouraging.

East passes again.

Your turn. Look at your hand again. You have an assortment of high cards. It looks as if you've got a reasonable chance at seven tricks all by yourself. Your partner would have passed if he did not have at least a few more. You want to get to game. You want to go for it. So far, your partner has committed you to a contract at the two level—eight tricks. But ten tricks means bonuses. Okay. How do we say this in bridge talk? 4♡! That describes your hand: "Before we sat down at the table, we agreed on the range of strength which one of us needed to make an opening bid of 1♡. We used an old-fashioned system that required that I have at least 'three and a half sure tricks.' You, my partner, don't know it, but I have a good deal more than the minimum of that range of strength. I am encouraged by your bid of 2♡. I am taking the plunge."

This is pretty unscientific. We are not being very precise. But we are making sense.

West passes. He tells his partner that he doesn't have enough strength to double. And he's not in a position to sacrifice.

North passes. He's said all that he can with his previous bid. He has no more power or information to offer.

East passes. She's in about the same shape as West.

The rest, we have already seen, is easy. West leads the ◇A (West is trying to get his diamond winners as quickly as he can.) The dummy is spread and the fit of the hands becomes clear. North and South make 4♡.

Let's look at a few more hands. How would you describe this one? (See page 64.)

> ♠ A 10 6
> ♡ K Q 8
> ◇ A K 10 6
> ♣ J 9 5

Let us answer this: "It looks as if I've got four sure tricks off the top—the ♠A, the ◇A, and ◇K, and either the ♡K or ♡Q. The ♣J might yield something. It also looks as if all of the cards are pretty evenly distributed in the suits, and the high cards are also scattered pretty evenly. It's a strong hand, but there is no suit that cries out to be named trump."

Question: How would you describe the hand in bridge code?

Answer: 1NT.

We have said that it is not actually necessary to have seven tricks in your own hand in order to make a "one" bid. How do you decide if you should open at all? That is, how do you decide if you have a rightful place in the auction? What is the level of strength that you should have?

Think about it. Most of the tricks are going to be taken by the high cards. We mean, specifically, the picture cards, or the "honors"—the aces, the kings, the queens, and the jacks. If you have a whole gallery of picture cards, your intuition will tell you that you have a rightful place in the auction. Even a nice assortment should draw you in. Making a "one" bid is your way of telling your partner that you have such a hand—that your hand has a rightful place in the auction.

An opening bidder who bids one of anything is saying, "Looking at my hand, I believe that if my partner holds an average hand, and particularly if we name the trump suit, we can take more tricks than they can." Anyone with a hand full of high cards is simply being rational by announcing, according to the code, that his team can probably take more tricks than the other team.

"A whole gallery" and "a nice assortment" are, admittedly, vague. Let's take some more steps toward precision.

Question: How many aces are there in the deck? How many kings? Queens? Jacks? How many high cards in all?

Answer: Four aces, four kings, four queens, and four jacks—for a total of sixteen high cards.

You are dealt this hand:

> ♠ A K J 9 5
> ♡ 10 9
> ◇ A 6 5 4
> ♣ K 10

Study it. Get it into your mind. You don't need to memorize it—just let the image of the hand register.

Question: Should you enter the auction?

Answer: Yes. You've got two aces. That's half the aces in the deck. Two kings. That's half the kings in the deck. One jack. That's a total of five high cards. And they are nice high cards. (You have fewer than seven sure tricks. Four, to be exact. But you should surely be in the auction.)

Question: If, by luck, everyone gets the same number of high cards, how many high cards will each hand have?

Answer: Four. There are sixteen high cards in the entire deck. Over the long haul, four is the average number of picture cards that you will see in a hand. Actually, the average is one of each—one ace, one king, one queen, one jack.

Look at the hand again:

> ♠ A K J 9 5
> ♡ 10 9
> ◇ A 6 5 4
> ♣ K 10

You have five high cards, more than your share. They are strong cards—two of them are aces and two of them are kings. You are rightfully in the auction. You have a hand that is well above average. That is not a vague assertion but a fact.

Question: How would you bid this hand?

Answer: 1♠. Spades is your longest and strongest suit. You would want spades to be trump. 1♠ is the perfect bid. The bid says that you have the kind of hand that warrants entering the bidding, and that spades is your suit.

Now put yourself in another situation. You are North. You and South have agreed that you will not open the bidding with less than an average hand. And, you have mapped out one definite agreement. If you open the bidding in a major suit (hearts or spades), you are assuring your partner that you have a least five cards in that suit.

South opens the bidding with 1♡. West passes. This is your hand and it's your turn:

North

♠ 7 3
♡ A Q 8 4
◇ 8 5
♣ K 9 6 4 2

In this situation, because your partner has already opened, your bid is "in response" to hers. You are "the responder." What would you bid?

Well, what do you want to say about your hand?

My high cards are less than average. I couldn't open the bidding with this hand. But I do have an ace and a king and a queen. And my partner has opened. She's got goodies. More than her share. She has described such a hand. She's looking for support. She bid 1♡—hearts are her suit. We have agreed that she must have five of them; therefore, we have a fit. My hearts now look very good. Nine trump! We need only eight for a fit.

Question: What "response" makes sense?

Answer: Bid 2♡. Exactly. We have not focused on the level of strength needed to join the auction as "responder," but once your partner has opened, you want to say that you do have high cards and that you can support hearts.

Let's look now at things from South's point of view. This is the hand that she opened, "One heart":

South

♠ A 5
♡ K 9 7 3 2
◇ A Q 9 7 6
♣ A

She has just heard her partner say, "Two hearts."

Bingo! South knows that they have found a trump fit.

Question: What is game in hearts?
Answer: 4♡. Ten tricks.
Here is South's hand again:

"2♡"

South

♠ A 5
♡ K 9 7 3 2
◇ A Q 9 7 6
♣ A

South can't see both hands, but North has given her a picture with his 2♡ bid—enough high cards to warrant chiming in, and he likes hearts. North would have passed, or bid something else, if he didn't have something like that. South thinks. Here is her analysis.

"North probably has ♡Q or ♡A, maybe both. That would give us a very good trump suit. That's probably at least four tricks.

"We will certainly take the black-suit aces. That's two more tricks.

"North might have another high card or two. Even if his high cards aren't in the trump suit, we are always in control with eight or more trump. His high cards will be somewhere and they will take tricks. In any suit, his cards will help to solidify what I hold.

"I have a good five-card diamond suit. Perhaps we can make extra tricks there.

"And if North is short in diamonds, there is a fair chance that I can take an extra trump trick by using one of North's hearts to trump one of my diamond losers, and make it into a winner.

"I have a very good hand, much better than average, and my partner has responded. By doing so, he has described a hand with some power, and has told me that it fits with my hearts. It looks as if we will have a play for ten tricks. Hearts is our suit! We can do it!"

So, after East bids or passes, South bids 4♡.

South's analysis was logical. In Chapter 10, we will be giving you specific tools to be much more systematic. You won't have to do this type of analysis every time you bid. The system will often tell you exactly what to bid, and you will trust it and see more and more why it makes sense. But it is crucial that you appreciate, now and during the rest of the book, that your bids never come out of thin air. And we want to assure you that sound logic, as well as tons of experience, lie behind the specifics of our system. The logic and the experience are embodied in it.

Look at this situation:

Dealer, South, opens with 1♣. You are West, the next bidder. This is your hand:

♠ K 6 4
♡ 10 9 7
◇ A K J 9 6
♣ 5 4

Question: Should you enter the auction?

Answer: Yes. You have four high cards, which is your share, and they are good ones. You have a very good suit. Definitely bid 1◇. That bid says a lot about your hand.

Note that you were not the opening bidder. Your bid was an "overcall." (You can "overcall" with less strength than you need to open the bidding. We will explain why later.)

Review:

To open the bidding   = An opening bid
To bid over your opponent's opening bid = An overcall
To respond to your partner's opening bid = A response

Question: West has passed, and North, your partner, opened with 1◇. This is your hand:

> ♠ 10 6 3 2
> ♡ 6 3 2
> ◇ 9 6 5 4
> ♣ 8 7

What would you bid?

Answer: "Pass" is the right bid here. It very accurately describes your hand. With no high cards, your hand is a "bust." Any other bid would mislead your partner.

9

A STEP-BY-STEP ANALYSIS OF A HAND

Question: South has opened 1♣. You are West. This is your hand:

♠ 9 8 6
♡ 9 8 7 6
♢ 10 7 4 2
♣ 9 8

What would you bid?
Answer: Definitely, "Pass." This hand is a bust. A stinkeroo.

Now it is North's turn. He bids 2♣ in response to South's opening 1♣ bid. He has support for his partner. It looks as if they have found a fit.

Then your partner, East, bids 2♠. Her bid tells you two things. One, she has a good spade suit. Two, she has more than minimal power, or she would not chime in now, at the two level, when you have passed and it looks as though North-South are going to win the auction.

Next, South bids 4♣. Here is a review of the bidding:

S	W	N	E
1♣	Pass	2♣	2♠
4♣			

Question: What does the 4♣ bid say to South's partner?

Answer: "I want to explore the possibility of game. Game in clubs is at the five level. I have more power than the minimum strength that my 1♣ opening bid promised, enough to jump to the four level, but not enough to jump all the way to 5♣ on my own. If you, North, also had extra values, more than the minimum that we agreed on for your response, when you supported me with 2♣, press on and bid to game. If not, pass."

Next, you (West) pass again.

Then North bids 5♣. He has decided to go for "game." It sounds as if he has the extra strength that South was looking for.

Finally, the bid is passed around. Here is a full review of the bidding:

S	W	N	E
1♣	Pass	2♣	2♠
4♣	Pass	5♣	Pass
Pass	Pass		

Question: How many tricks has North contracted his partnership to take?

Answer: Eleven tricks. A 5♣ bid—a bid at the "five level"—is a bid to take eleven tricks.

All players get their share of bust hands. Grin and bear them. Did you notice the ◇10 in your hand? That might be the difference between 5♣ made and 5♣ down. Hang on

to your ◇10. East overcalled. North and South may well
have overbid.

Let's look at all of the hands:

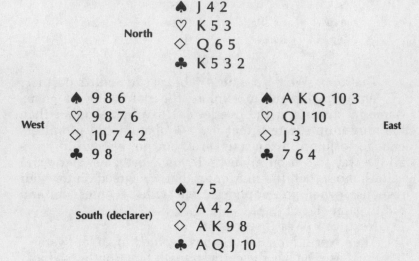

North-South must take eleven tricks. That's a lot of
tricks—all of the tricks except two. You want to defeat the
contract, which is the same thing as saying that you want to
"set" the contract.

Question: How many tricks do you and your partner
have to take to set the contract? Can you think of another
way of saying that a contract has been set?

Answer: Three tricks. Three defensive tricks will cause
your opponents to go "down one." Four tricks will cause
them to go "down two," and so on.

Question: Don't look back at the diagram. Who is the
opening leader? Who plays the first card?

Answer: You are. You do. West. South first named clubs.
You sit to her left, clockwise from her.

Question: What would you lead?

Answer: Spades! (The ♠9 looks nice.) Your partner bid them. If the defense has tricks anywhere, they should be in spades. In fact, your alert partner, realizing early in the bidding that it was North-South's hand, made her 2♠ bid for the very purpose of telling you what to lead. In defending against trump contracts, it is often a good idea to take your winners in your suit as soon as you can, before the declarer discards his or her losers in your suit and then . . .

Question: . . . does what?

Answer: Trumps your or your partner's beauties.

Getting back to the hand, do you think that North-South will make it, or that they will go down? Let's switch to South's point of view. Don't look at the East-West cards now. When the dummy is laid down, South will see only the opening lead and her own and her partner's hands.

Look the situation over for a while until you have a good sense of the lie of the cards:

	♠ J 4 2
North	♡ K 5 3
(dummy)	◇ Q 6 5
	♣ K 5 3 2

"♠9"

	♠ 7 5
South	♡ A 4 2
(declarer)	◇ A K 9 8
	♣ A Q J 10

Here is a very good approach. When playing a suit contract, as opposed to a No-Trump contract, you should focus the analysis of where the tricks will come from by counting losers first. When we analyzed a previous hand, we know that we concentrated on identifying, directly, your winning pairs. But the fact is that, if you focus first on losers, which should be fewer, the winners will then emerge easily.

One very good way to do this is to focus on one hand. Focus on South. See if each of her losing cards can be paired with a definite winner in North's hand. If not, you've identified a possible loser. You have also identified the problem areas of the play.

North-South are going to lose some spade tricks, aren't they? Your assay reveals the weakness in that suit very quickly. Two spade losers. One possible heart loser. One possible diamond loser. South has her work cut out for her. She could be off one. Maybe two.

Now, let's shift points of view again. You are back as West. We will peek back into South's strategy soon.

Let's look at one possible play of this hand, step by step.

This is a very important exercise. Really pay attention here.

Tricks one and two: You have led ♠9. On the first two tricks, your partner, East, goes high with the ♠Q and then leads the ♠K for two defensive tricks.

Now the hand looks like this:

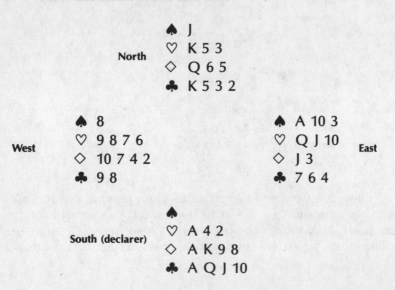

Question: Who has the lead?

Answer: East. She won the last trick.

Trick three: East leads the ♠A. It is a "safe lead." She has taken two spade tricks. She doesn't know where her next trick is coming from. She can't see any other lead that will help her. She won't give anything away by leading her suit, even though South will probably trump it now. (There is also the chance, from the point of view of East, who can't see your hand, that you, West, started with only two spades, and you will get the trump trick and defeat the contract.)

Declarer "ruffs" (another word for "trumps") with the ♣10 from his hand. You and North follow suit.

Three tricks played. Score: Defense 2, Declarer 1.

Here is how the situation looks now:

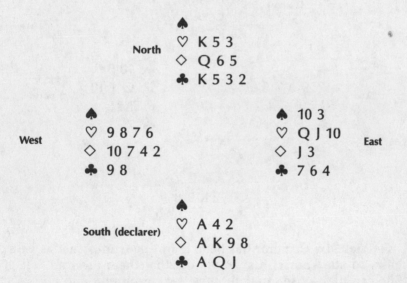

North
♠
♡ K 5 3
◇ Q 6 5
♣ K 5 3 2

West
♠
♡ 9 8 7 6
◇ 10 7 4 2
♣ 9 8

East
♠ 10 3
♡ Q J 10
◇ J 3
♣ 7 6 4

South (declarer)
♠
♡ A 4 2
◇ A K 9 8
♣ A Q J

Tricks four and five: On trick four, declarer leads the ♣A and wins the trick. Then, on the next trick, she plays the ♣Q to win the trick.

Question: What is declarer up to?

Answer: She is pulling trumps. She wants to get those dangerous cards out of the defenders' hands. You and East have to follow suit.

That's five tricks.

Question: How many rounds of trump have been played?

Answer: Two. Everyone has followed suit on two trump leads. Eight trump cards have fallen. And don't forget, declarer used a trump when she "ruffed" East's third round of spades. That's nine. There are four trump left. Count 'em. Now the hand looks like this:

Dummy
♠
♡ K 5 3
◇ Q 6 5
♣ K 5

You
♠
♡ 9 8 7 6
◇ 10 7 4 2
♣

Your partner
♠ 10 3
♡ Q J 10
◇ J 3
♣ 7

Declarer
♠
♡ A 4 2
◇ A K 9 8
♣ J

Trick six: Declarer has been counting trump, just as we have, so she knows, just as we do, that there are four left. She can plainly see that she has two in dummy and one in her hand. It follows, as the night follows the day, that you and East have one trump left between you, although declarer, who does not have the benefit of the diagram, does not know whether it is held by you or East. She doesn't care. She leads the ♣J from her hand, knowing that the defenders' last trump must fall.

After each hand plays a card, the situation looks like this:

	Dummy	
	♠	
	♡ K 5 3	
	◇ Q 6 5	
	♣ K	

You		**Your partner**
♠		♠ 10 3
♡ 9 8 7		♡ Q J 10
◇ 10 7 4 2		◇ J 3
♣		♣

	Declarer	
	♠	
	♡ A 4 2	
	◇ A K 9 8	
	♣	

Notice that only dummy has a trump left. Declarer has drawn all the trump from both your hand and West's. Another way to say this is she has "pulled trump."

On this sixth trick, you, West, were the hand that was out of trumps. You had to discard. We made the discard for you.

Question: Try to find the next answer in your mind, without looking back to the diagrams. What card did you discard?

Try it. Once you have given it some time, whether or not you think you know, look back and compare the last two diagrams. Firm up your answer. Then look at our answer.

Answer: ♡6.

Tricks seven and eight: Declarer plays to the ♡K in dummy by leading her small heart from her hand. She then plays the last trump, ♣K, discarding the ♡4 from her hand. You and East follow suit with ♡7 and ♡10 on trick seven and must both discard on trick eight. East discards ♠3. You discard ♡8.

Eight tricks played. Score: Defense 2, Declarer 6.

Declarer seems to be gaining on you. How did she do this? Remember, she pulled trumps in three rounds. She took the ♣10 as an individual trump trick on trick two. Now, she has used the ♣K in dummy as an individual trick, on which she discarded a losing heart from her hand. Five trump winners. Oh what those trumps can do for you! We thought that South might go down two. Now, it looks as though she really means business. She has solved the problem of a possible heart loser. And it is pretty obvious that she is going to try to avoid a diamond loser as well.

The situation looks like this:

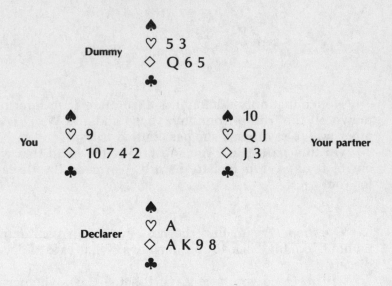

Dummy
♠
♡ 5 3
♢ Q 6 5
♣

You
♠
♡ 9
♢ 10 7 4 2
♣

Your partner
♠ 10
♡ Q J
♢ J 3
♣

Declarer
♠
♡ A
♢ A K 9 8
♣

Trick nine: Declarer is in the dummy. Another way to say this is she is "on the board." On the ninth trick, she plays to the ♡A in her hand by leading a small heart from dummy. You and East follow suit. Now it looks like this:

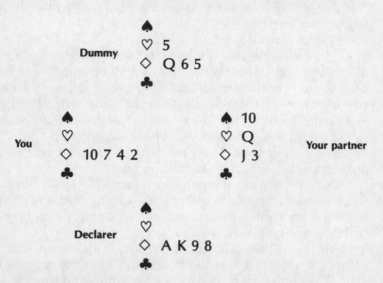

Four cards left. Declarer takes a very good look at the cards that she can see. She still needs all the remaining tricks. She can't see your cards. This is what she can see:

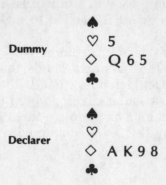

The ♢AKQ are good. That is three more winners. Where is that other winner going to come from?

From the ♢9.

What! Declarer knows that she doesn't have the ♢J or ♢10, so defenders must. How can she think that the ♢9 might take a trick?

She has two hopes:

Although she does not know which defender has which diamonds, she does know that no diamonds have been played, and that you and East have six of them. If each of you has three of them—if they "split"—she will draw them just as she drew trump. She will win the first three diamond rounds with ♢A, ♢K, and ♢Q. Those rounds will "pull" the defenders' diamonds. Then her fourth diamond will be the only diamond left. The ♢9 will be good.

But suppose she doesn't have a favorable split? Suppose the diamonds in your hand and East's are split 4–2. When there are six cards out in a suit, the 4–2 split is mathematically more likely than 3–3.

All is not lost. She can still hope, in that case, that the defender with only two diamonds has both the ♢J and the ♢10. They will "drop" on the first two diamond rounds, and her ♢9 will still be "good."

Before we go on explaining this hand, we want to point out that there will be times in this book when, instead of referring to a specific card, we will simply use an "x." That means that no particular card is needed to make that particular point.

So, to continue this lesson, declarer wins if the diamonds "split" evenly in the defenders' hands, that is, if there are three diamonds in each defender's hand. In this hand, it doesn't matter which particular diamonds are in which of the defenders' hands, as long as there are three in each.

Another way to say this is—declarer wins if the diamonds "split"

xxx–xxx

In this hand, declarer will also win if the diamonds split
xxxx–J10
or
J10–xxxx
She doesn't see other strategies. She might as well play
for one of her dreams to come true.

Again, here are all of the cards at this point:

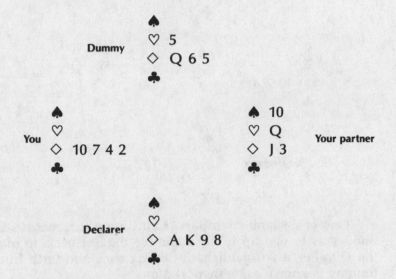

Trick ten: Declarer plays ◇K from her hand and ◇5
from dummy. You and East follow suit.

Ten tricks played. Score: Defense 2, Declarer 8.

Question: Where is declarer?

Answer: Still in her hand. She just won with ♢K in her hand. Now it looks like this:

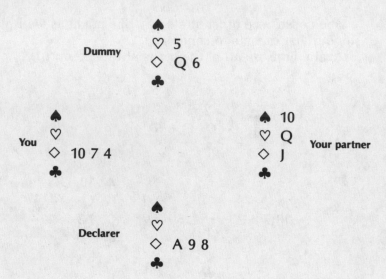

One of declarer's winners is sitting on the board: ♢Q. She wants to end up in her hand for the last trick, to play the ♢9 after it is established. Getting back and forth from dummy is known as "transportation."

High-density significant lesson: South now does a little thinking about "transportation." She knows that she had better be careful. "Transportation" is crucial. If she doesn't plan ahead, she could make a mistake: taking the ♢A now and the ♢Q on the twelfth trick. She would then be in dummy. She would be stuck in dummy! It would look like this when it was time to play the thirteenth trick:

♠

♡ 5   **Declarer would**

◇ (Q!! = last winner)   **be here!!**

♣

♠

♡

◇ 9

♣

Even if everything worked out for her, and the ◇9 was established, if she innocently started to play the ◇9 from her hand, some wily defender, namely your partner, East, who had been holding on to her hearts, would say sweetly, "You're on the board, Drilla," which is the very same thing as saying, "You're in dummy. You must play from dummy." Declarer would have to play ♡5, a loser, for down one!

The ◇9 will be good only if South can get to it when she wants to. Declarer is "worrying about transportation," and she is wise to do so.

Siren! Alarm! If you have not slowly digested the last three paragraphs and tested your understanding of them with the diagram, go back! It is teeming with goodies. If you have digested it, then you have learned more bridge than you ever thought you would. We will never again in this book announce a siren alarm.

Declarer has thought through the transportation. Now she grows even more cunning. She figures that even if she doesn't get her favorable split, one or both of the defenders might blow it and make it all easy! They might just toss out that ◇J or ◇10. "Let's make them discard. Let's give them a chance to make a mistake. Let's take it one slow trick at a time."

Trick eleven: She forgoes the ◇A. She plays her ◇8 to the dummy's ◇Q. Everyone follows suit.

Well, well, well! East played the ◇J.

"What does it mean," declarer asks herself. "Why did East play the ◇J? That is the highest diamond the defenders have. Maybe that was her last diamond. If so, since this is the second round of diamonds, I know that diamonds were originally split

10xxx–Jx

and my dreams are shattered. I needed

xxx–xxx
or
xxxx–J10
or
J10–xxxx.

"I know I haven't seen the ◇10. Someone is holding on to that ◇10. East is sweet, but she is cunning, too. She might have started with J10x and she played the ◇J just to make me wonder. To rattle me. Just to make me sweat for my contract. I just took ◇Q. I'm on the board. As if I would accidentally play the ♡5 now!

"Stick to the program. Actually, I really don't have much of a choice. Let's get optimistic. All I have to do is play ◇6, which will take me nicely back to my hand and ◇A, and then ◇9 will cozy me home. 5♣ bid and made."

Trick twelve: South calls for the ◇6 from dummy.

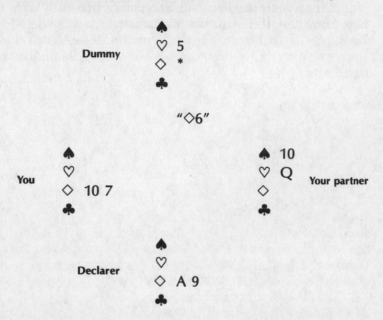

South holds her breath. East shows out—East plays
♠10. The diamonds have split, after all:

10xxx–Jx

South lays down ◇A. You play ◇7, holding on to ◇10 as if
it were a life preserver.

Trick thirteen: South is in her hand with her last diamond, for which she had had so much hope, but which, she now knows, will not do the job for her:

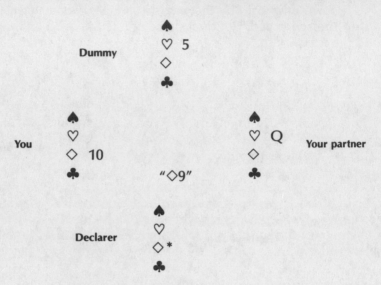

You, West, smile and cover with your ◇10, taking the trick.

Let's say a few kind words for the ◇7. Oh yes. Without the ◇7, and those other two little diamonds (do you remember them—the ◇4 and ◇2?), you, West, sitting patiently with your "bust" hand, could never have held on to the ◇10. It would have been "pulled." But you were right to hold on to ◇10, to clasp it and cherish it. It turned out to be the setting trick. Declarer hoped that you'd make a mistake. Actually, you made the key decision to hold on to diamonds at trick six, which was the first time that you had to discard, and you discarded the ♡6.

A new deck is opened, because you have squeezed the poor ◇10 so hard that the diamonds have been crushed into sand. The rest is history.

5♣ was bid. North-South held powerful cards. Tricks: Declarer ten, Defenders three. Declarer took many tricks, but one less than her team contracted for.

Down one! And by the way, those ten tricks never make it to the score pad. Contract defeated! That's what makes it to the score pad.

That's the fascinating equipoise of the game of bridge.

Question: Can you think of another term for "down one" or "set one trick"?

Answer: "Off one." You may have noticed that we used the expression as part of the lesson, without explaining it. Maybe you learned the expression in context, without even noticing.

This very painstaking examination of the play of a bridge hand was worth it. Many of the situations you encountered will arise again and again, and you will recognize them, even though they may wear different clothes. You have learned the ideas behind the specific plays. You have learned a lot.

10

BIDDING: THE SYSTEM

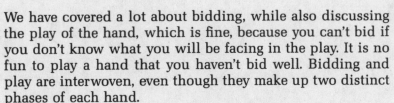

We have covered a lot about bidding, while also discussing the play of the hand, which is fine, because you can't bid if you don't know what you will be facing in the play. It is no fun to play a hand that you haven't bid well. Bidding and play are interwoven, even though they make up two distinct phases of each hand.

Remember what we illustrated with the 5♣ contract, down one. *Pass* can be a very good bid, and the passing hand may contain an inconsequential-looking, but dynamite, card.

In the last few chapters, we have taught you the logic that lies behind bidding, a way to think about bidding. Everything that we have said thus far has really been no more than the application of logical thought to the rules of a specific card game.

The bridge auction was invented and is geared to search logically for the best contract. But remember, because bids are imperfect tools, you cannot always make the "one true bid," but, rather, you must make the best bid available, as you sit at the table holding certain cards. And, sometimes, a very well bid hand will face an array of cards that will defeat it. That is to be expected. All good bids are based on a logic of probabilities, and the probabilities don't always work for you. But good bids work most of the time.

So far, we have not used a bidding code, or system. The bids in the last chapters, which were arrived at fairly and intuitively, were good bids. Those bids met our responsibility to the cards to describe them well. Still, no one would use a solely intuitive method of bidding to arrive at each and every bid, despite the fact that the logic behind each bid might be sound and the bid responsibly descriptive.

You and your partner have the opportunity to adopt an agreed-upon code. This code—this understanding between you—will be designed to make your bids more precise. We do not suggest you make one up from scratch. Very few people ever do that.

We are sure that your time would best be spent, and your enjoyment maximized, if you adopted our system. Virtually everyone, including experts and professionals, uses this system. As much as any system around, it will give you a solid framework to look at your hands, to think about your options, and to describe your hands. Many times, it will be right on the money. When this system tells you to make a certain bid holding certain cards at a certain time, then you should do so. Not only will it work to get you to the best contract, but, after all, you have agreed with your partner to use that code.

But before we delve into the specifics—remember: The system is only the superstructure of your bids. No system can tell you exactly what to bid on every hand, every time your turn to bid comes around. Bids are coded information, not final resting places.

BIDDING FIVE-CARD MAJORS

Spades and hearts are called the major suits. Ten tricks ("four spades" or "four hearts") is game.

Diamonds and clubs are called the minor suits. Tricks in those suits are worth fewer points. It takes eleven tricks ("five diamonds" or "five clubs") to make game.

The core of the system can be summed up in two sentences: Open with a major suit bid (spades or hearts) if you have *five* or more cards in that suit, and sufficient total high-card strength, including some ace or king in your hand. If you have sufficient strength, but you do not have a five-card major suit, bid your minor suit.

Always bid the longer suit first.

If the minor suits are equal in length, bid the stronger.

With two five-card majors, always open the bidding with one spade.

The overarching rule is: Open with a five-card major.

> With
> ♠ A
> ♡ K 9 7 6 5
> ◇ Q 10 9 7 4 3
> ♣ A
>
> Open 1♡.

With	With
♠ K J 9 7 4	♠ K J 9 7 4
♡ A 10 8 7 3 2	♡ A 10 8 7 3
◇ A	◇ A
♣ 9	♣ 9 2
Open 1♡.	Open 1♠.

These rules may seem arbitrary now. They are very helpful at the table. We will review them fully in Chapter 13. It is time to start focusing clearly on the *shape* of your hand.

Don't memorize this. Focus on how much you tell your partner with "1♠":

(1) I have sufficient high-card strength, an ace or a king, and
(2) my hand looks something like

this:	or this:	or this:
♠ xxxxx	♠ xxxxx	♠ xxxxxx
♡ xxxxx	♡ xxxx	♡ xxxxx
◇ xx	◇ xx	◇ xx
♣ x	♣ xx	♣

not this:	*not* this:	*not* this:	*not* this:
♠ xxxx	♠ xxxxx	♠ xxx	♠ xx
♡ xxxxx	♡ xxxxxx	♡ xxxx	♡ xxxxx
◇ xxx	◇ x	◇ x	◇ xxxxxx
♣ x	♣ x	♣ xxxxx	♣

Question: Assuming sufficient strength, what would you open with the last four hands?

Answer: 1♡   1♡   1♣   1♡!

Readers who have played before, and even some readers who have learned recently, were taught to open with a four-card major suit. Experience has shown that our system will help you get to the right contract with hands that were difficult to describe with the old system. Most important, our system's emphasis is on helping you to find more fits in 4♡ and 4♠, which are the two best game contracts from the point of view of play of the hand. The change will be very easy to adapt to, and the rewards will be great.

Readers who have played before will also notice that there are codes that they have heard about or used that are not used in this book. For example, some players use an opening "two bid" to describe a weak hand. In this book, an opening "two bid" describes a strong hand. You have to choose one or the other meaning for your code. Our choice is more common and works better overall. There are also codes for certain situations that do not appear in this book because they tend to be confusing for the beginner or do not work as well. This book will give you an inventory of codes that will get you to good contracts, will allow you to use your brain, and will be fun to use.

Some readers will also have heard of "duplicate bridge," or tournament bridge, involving many tables. In duplicate bridge, a sorting device is used so that all of the tables play all of the same hands. All North-South teams compete against all North-South teams. All East-West teams compete against all East-West teams. The scoring is different than in rubber bridge, which this book is about. But the game is very much the same.

SUFFICIENT STRENGTH

Look at this hand:

> ♠ A Q 10
> ♡ A K 4 3 2
> ◇ A 6
> ♣ 7 5 3

Is it a good hand? Is it a bad hand? You are at the point where just a glance will tell you it's a pretty nice hand.

How would you describe it in words? You could say that it has this and that card, so many hearts, so many clubs, and so on. That doesn't evaluate the hand. That just says what you see. Just the same, in any endeavor, you are often alerted to a great deal simply by stating carefully what you observe. It can be a valuable starting point.

You might want to get a little more emotional: "Those three aces fill me up. That ace-king is very, very nice." That is evaluative but vague.

Or you might want to do as we did in the last chapter. You might want to come up with some way to make a rational assessment of the trick-taking power, based on some system of grading. You could observe that ♡AK will give you two tricks, that the ♠A and ♢A are also definites, and that the ♠Q is a genuine maybe. If you look at the hand from the point of trick-taking power, four definite tricks and one genuine maybe is more than your share.

You could assign a bid to describe such a hand: 1♠ = four definite tricks and one genuine maybe.

You could count the number of your high cards. You have five. As we saw in the last chapter, five high cards are more than your share. You could assign a bid: 1♠ = more than my share of high cards. That would not be very precise. It could mean four aces and one king. It could mean one queen and four jacks.

Of the four—"I'm lookin' at em," "I'm having an emotional reaction to 'em," "I'm spotting tricks," and "I'm countin' 'em"—the last two, of course, make the most sense. Still, communicating to your partner that you have "more than my share" or "genuine maybes" can get very awkward and vague. It's not that these valuations aren't descriptive. But they are still too vague.

These are modern times. We like to express everything in numbers. Today, practically every bridge player in the world uses a method of numbers to evaluate his or her hand and to put it into perspective. This is not a method of scoring. You do it in your head when you bid. Each high card is assigned a point value, and counting up your points is called "point count."

Each A is assigned the value of 4 high-card points.

K	3
Q	2
J	1

Question: How many high-card points are there in each suit and in the entire deck? How many high-card points are "my share"? How many are "more than my share"?

Answer: There are 10 high-card points in each suit and 40 in the deck. My share is 10. More than my share is 11 or more.

Don't let us mislead you, however. In the hands in the last chapters, all of the opening bidders had more than 11 high-card points. You will see that you need a little more than your "share" to open the bidding. Actually, you need *twelve* high-card points.

Look at this hand:

> KJx
> QJxxx
> AJx
> 10x

Question: How many high-card points does it have?
Answer: 12.

So far, all that the points do is permit you to think of a hand in terms of a number. It's easy and convenient. But we have to go further and show you how counting points will lead you to the best bid.

The connection between point count and bid is this:

We now know how many *combined* high-card points in your hand and your partner's hand will give you a real shot at taking seven tricks. We also know the *combined* point count necessary for a partnership to make a "two" bid. We know these *combined* point-count levels right on up to a "seven" bid—and thirteen tricks.

How do we know these things? Years of experience, around the globe, have tested and verified the connections between levels of points and levels of trick-taking power. Point count works. Its reliability in predicting the "makability" of a contract has not been established by a rigorous statistical study. It has been established by the rigorous scrutiny of people who hate to lose contracts.

By the same token, looking at it from the perspective of just one hand, it is now known how many high-card points are needed to make a responsible opening bid. Experience shows that it is unwise to open the bidding with fewer than 12 high-card points.

Question: With two kings, four queens, and two jacks, how many high-card points do you have? Is it enough to open?

Answer: 16. Yes.

If you open the bidding with fewer than 12 high-card points, you're going to find yourself going down more times than you like. It's a game of inches.

We also can see that point count makes sense, not only by experience, but by simple logic. For example, you and your partner need 37 combined points to bid a grand slam. If you have 36, then the defenders have 4—either an ace, or its trick-taking equivalent. You can't take all the tricks. For another example, how many combined points does your partnership need to bid a small slam? 33. If you have 32 high-card points, then the defenders have 8, the equivalent of two aces.

You might be suspecting by now (and you would be correct) that in our system your bids will be describing your point-count strength within a given range. Just as an example, 1NT means, "I have 15 to 17 high-card points and an evenly distributed hand." 1NT is one of the most exact of the bids—fifteen to seventeen, no less, no more. It is a precise statement of strength within exact lower and upper limits.

Does this mean that you are going to have to catalog in your head a hundred bids and their numerical meanings? No! Heaven forbid. You will just have to focus on the point-count requirements of a few crucial bids. You will see these bids in terms of the crucial combined point-count level necessary to make certain contracts. They will act as markers in the system. Then, everything else will fall into place. We will come to that later. Don't let us get away with anything. We have promised you

- crucial bids
- crucial combined point-count levels

We will keep these promises in Chapters 13 and 17.

On page 90, we related the core of our system in two sentences. Here is part of that core—the first sentence—but, this time, refined and stated in terms of point count: Open with a major-suit bid (♡ or ♠) if you have a five-card major suit and 12 high-card points, including some ace or king.

That is, 12 high-card points, including an ace or king = "sufficient high-card strength" to open a five-card major suit.

Question: What would you bid with this hand if you were the first bidder?:

> ♠ A Q 8
> ♡ Q 7 6 3 2
> ◇ A Q 7
> ♣ 7 5

Answer: 1♡.

Question: Righty deals and passes and it is your turn. What would you bid with this hand?:

> ♠ A Q 3
> ♡ K 6 5 4 3
> ◇ J 7 6
> ♣ 5 2

Answer: Pass. You have insufficient high-card strength to open.

Question: Would you open the bidding with this hand?:

> ♠ A J 5 2
> ♡ 9
> ◇ K Q J 9 8
> ♣ Q 7 5

Answer: Yes. Good answer. But not 1♠. You have only four spades. If you think that the bid is 1◇, your instincts and/or your memory are good. The second sentence of the core of our system is: If you do have sufficient strength, but you do not have a five-card major suit, bid your minor suit.

Question: Would you open with either of these hands?:

♠ A 10
♡ A K 6
◇ 7 5
♣ A K J 10 8 7

♠ A J 7 5 2
♡ K 10 9 4
◇ A 10 5
♣ 9

Answer: Yes. Both of them. 1♣. 1♠.

DISTRIBUTION POINTS

Besides high-card points, many hands that are played in suit (trump) contracts have other special values that we also express in terms of points.

Look at these hands of North-South:

North
♠ A 7 5 3
♡ J 9 7 5
◇ K 8
♣ 6 4 2

South
♠ K Q J 9 8 4 2
♡ 10
◇ A J 6
♣ J 3

North and South have eleven trumps between them. This means that East and West will have only two trumps. If each has one trump, the defenders will be stripped of their trumps on the first trump round. If one of them has both trumps, then the defenders' trumps will be "drawn" or "pulled" in two rounds. Either way, once declarer draws trumps, all the rest of the trumps will be good, even the itty-bitty two.

Declarer has length in his suit. Length! That is the magic word. Length is good. Length can be wonderful. All those tiny trump cards turn into "little jewels." Length has value. *Length is strength.*

Looking at length in your trump suit is one method of focusing on the "distribution" of your cards. "Distribution" can create power. Another method of focusing on distributional values is to look at the shortness in your side suits. Both methods are windows on the same room.

Read what follows not to memorize but to shake your head in agreement and say, "Well, of course. That makes simple sense."

If you deal any thirteen cards, they will necessarily be "distributed" into suits.

This is an example of suit distribution:

Kxxx   AQJ   109x   KQx

That is "even" or "balanced" distribution. (It is also a perfect example of a 1NT bid, as you will recognize if you have been playing close attention.) If you count just the number of cards in each suit, you could call that hand a "4-3-3-3." That is the pattern in which the suits are distributed.

Every hand must be distributed in some way to add up to thirteen. For example, if you think about it, you will see that if you have xxxxx in any one suit, you will have to have at least one suit with no more than xx.

Look at this hand—a clear example of shortness in a side suit:

♠ A Q J 7 5 3
♡ A 10 2
◇ A 6 4
♣ 3

It looks as if your hand won't be taking any tricks in clubs. But even if your partner has no strength in clubs, you know that if you play the hand in spades, you won't lose many club tricks. In fact, you will lose only one club trick.

Question: Why is that?

Answer: Because after you lose one club trick, you will trump any other club rounds. What you don't have—additional losing clubs—is valuable. After one round of clubs, you will be in control of the suit.

So, shortness in a side suit adds value to your hand, as does length in your trump suit.

Focusing on "shortness" is the more reliable method of accurately translating the distributional values of your hand into point count. We know this by experience. So, if you want to evaluate your distributional values, you have to look at your "short" suits.

Here are three new words:

A void   = no cards in a side suit
A singleton = one card in a side suit
A doubleton = two cards in a side suit

These distributional values can be expressed in point count. In our system:

A void   adds 3 points to your high-card points
A singleton adds 2
A doubleton adds 1

You can see that point count indicates that in a suit contract, a void may be very valuable. It means that you have length somewhere else. It also means that if the defenders lead that suit, which they very well might, you can trump and get control.

Look at this hand:

> ♠ A J 7 5 3
> ♡ K J 10
> ◇ K 7 6
> ♣ 4 3

How many high-card points does it have? 12. How many distribution points does it have? One—the club doubleton. How many high-card points and distribution points does it have? 13.

Question: If you have a trump-type hand, a singleton in a side suit is worth how many points? A void is worth how many points? A doubleton is worth how many points?
Answer: A singleton is worth 2, a void 3, and a doubleton one.

Question:

> ♠ K 9 6 4
> ♡ Q J 5 4
> ◇
> ♣ A K J 7 3

How many high-card points do you have? How many distribution points?
Answer: 14, 3.

Question: How many total points repose in each of the following hands?

> 1. ♠ 8 6
>   ♡ A J 7 6 3
>   ◇ K J 6
>   ♣ K 9 7

2. ♠ Q J 9
   ♡ A K 6 4
   ◇ K 7 5 2
   ♣ 10 6

3. ♠ A K 9
   ♡ A Q J 10 6
   ◇ A K 6
   ♣ 10 5

Answer: 1. 13, 2. 14, 3. 22.

Question: Here's the last hand again:

♠ A K 9
♡ A Q J 10 6
◇ A K 6
♣ 10 5

Does your evaluation tell you that you definitely intend to play the hand with hearts as trump?

Answer: No. You would want to play this hand with hearts as trump only if your partner had a fit with you. Does partner have any hearts? We don't know yet.

Question: If you were the dealer with this hand, would you open the bidding?

♠ 6
♡ A Q J 7 2
◇ K Q 8
♣ 10 7 6 5

Answer: Yes. 1♡. Absolutely. You have 12 high-card points and a "five-card or longer" major suit. You have "some ace or king" (♡A, ◇K); 1♡ describes the hand as well as it can be described, according to the core of our system.

A few pages ago we asked you to check out the fact that in every hand in which you have a suit with five cards (xxxxx), you will have at least one suit with no more than two (xx). You now know another way to say this: Every hand with a five-card suit will have at least one void, singleton, or doubleton.

A hand with a five-card suit has a shape that we know is good for playing. *A hand with a five-card major suit and 12 high-card points automatically has at least one distributional point, or 13 total points.*

Question: How many total points repose in each of the following hands?

1. ♠ 10 9 8 7 2
   ♡ 10 3
   ◇ A K 4
   ♣ A J 8

2. ♠ A Q J 9 4
   ♡ Q J 10
   ◇ Q 5 3
   ♣ 8 4

Answer: 1. 13, 2. 13.

Trick Question: How many total points are there in this hand?

♠ A 10 9 6 4
♡ A 8 7 3 2
◇ J 5
♣ A

Answer: 15! We know that we have to clarify this. The problem areas are:

♣A—we count this as 6 points.
◇J5—we count this as 1 point.

The club singleton ace is powerful. It is an ace. You have control in the suit immediately. You will get a sure trick, and you won't use a trump. You have no losers in the suit. Your evaluation of strength should reflect that when it comes to side suits, a singleton ace is a topper.

As to A, Ax, and Kx, count both the high-card points and the distribution points.

A = 6 total points
Ax = 5
Kx = 4

Actually, in this chapter we are discussing the minimum strength needed to open, and we are focusing on high cards. The question is usually: Do I have the high-card strength to enter the auction?

Still, you should pay close attention to distributional values. They are very important in getting a sense of your hand. But the fear of bridge teachers is that players get hung up on "counting points," fail to appreciate the *shape* of their hand, and forget that distribution points are a way of giving credit to the fact that certain shaped hands are good for playing.

THE BORDERLINE

The real issue about distributional values in the first round of the auction arises when it is now your turn, no one has opened, and you are considering opening. Your hand looked kind of average as you picked it up and arranged it, and when you focus you see that your doubleton or singleton is made up of an unprotected honor: K, Qx, Q, Jx, J. Asking yourself, "Do I count Jx as a high-card point *and* a doubleton point?" shows that you are getting responsible about describing your hand. But the issue in your mind is not really one about whether you will have control after two rounds of the suit. You will. The real issue is whether the unprotected jack has a realistic chance of taking a trick. Over the long run, when you play, some will and some won't take tricks. What is certain is that you are making too much of the holding if you count both its trick-taking potential and its "shortness" value.

Point count is a *tool* for evaluating your hand and for communicating, to be used wisely. Wondering how many points to assign to Jx is not an abstract riddle—it is a way of focusing on the reality of the jack's trick-taking value.

Let us give you some clear rules. When evaluating your hand as to whether to open, count these as high cards only— over the long haul, they will work for you:

$$K \quad Q \quad Qx \quad Jx$$

Don't count the singleton J as a high card when you are tallying the 12 points needed to open. It is way too iffy as a high card. It is a singleton, period. It is wonderful. Truly. The singleton will help you control the suit. But it is unlikely to take a trick.

Look at this hand:

> AKxxx
> KJx
> xxxx
> J

No system is perfect. All general rules eventually cry out for exceptions. The above hand does not meet the guidelines for opening, since the J can not be counted as a high card. Yet you have two sure tricks, whereas in this hand, which does meet the rules:

AQxxx

KJx

xxx

Qx

You have only one sure trick. It still remains the case that there is nothing to fear but fear itself. Open with this hand. It will play well in a fit with your partner. But open with a sense of the cards. (Experienced bridge players, we must admit, would open with the first hand as well.)

We shudder that you might decide that we want you to approach the bidding like a number-happy automaton. Doubletons and singletons and voids are good for you only if you also have the foundation of viable high cards and trumps to take tricks.

You are not a robot. As important as bidding rules are, they are not engraved in stone. There are hands when you must apply them first, and then toss them aside. Look at this hand:

Axxxxxxxx

Jx

K

Q

Only your mind, and your attention to the bidding, are going to lead you to describe these cards wisely.

Once you begin to play, you will see hands with fewer points that "play nicely" in certain combinations with your partner. After a while you will add this knowledge of cards and your growing sixth sense to the auction. You will see that KQJx is not just six points but also a nice combination to hold. Still, until you feel on very solid ground, stick to the guidelines. In the overwhelmingly high number of hands, if you use the guidelines, you will usually get to the right contract. You won't miss game and slam opportunities. You will always be in the ballpark.

We would never say that we are giving you hard and fast rules for every situation. We are giving you rules to learn by, and we do want you to use them. But we also know that, in every hand, bidding calls on your judgment and your sense of "playability." This will grow as you read on and as you play. In some suits, for example ◇AJ1094, a 10 and 9 can be very important and can sway a close bidding decision. The real doubt that arises is about your partner's expectations. A rule of thumb might be to bid conservatively when a new situation arises, but to make a mental note to discuss the holding with your partner after the hand. Then you are really playing bridge.

The point is: Follow our rule for opening bids. But always think. If you see a hand (and there won't be many) where you feel that the rule just does not seem to guide you to where you are comfortable, then your intuition is probably well grounded. And that is excellent news. It means that you are trying responsibly to describe your hand. You will be playing bridge. We wish you good luck and fun. Any game that could be totally captured in general rules could get boring. If you hold Qx, you have a right to wonder if you have a viable high card. It would *certainly* be viable if, later in the bidding, your partner bid the suit, because his or her suit would give your queen the protection it needs. But without that reassuring bid, you should not be astonished that your sleeve is being tugged by your intuition, and that it is asking you to take closer look at all of your suits, because you'll be looking at a high card on the borderline. Still, you'd rather have Qx than 9x.

Well into your bridge career, you might open with a hand like this:

♠ K J x x x
♡ x x
◇ A Q x x x
♣ x

This hand has only 10 high-card points. It also has two good suits, and it is very "playable" if your partner has a fit in either suit. But it is not for now. Opening with this hand would violate our rule.

Stick with our rule and watch the results. No system, however good, is perfect. No system can cover every deal. And nobody is smart enough to imagine every deal in advance.

♠

♡

♢

♣

11
HAVE A (TRUMP) FIT

By this time you are starting to see the pieces of a bidding system fitting together. You know that we are concentrating on length in the trump suit, on high-card points, on distributional points, and on "fit." We already covered "trump fit." It can't hurt to have a refresher. How many cards should my partner and I have, together, in our trump suit? The answer is *at least eight!!!!!*

You probably don't get the sense that we are middle-of-the-road on this component in our system.

4 in my hand and 4 in partner's hand	= nice
5	3	= quite acceptable
6	2	= sure
7	1	= just fine
8	0	= yes, it's like having a 4–4 fit in your own hand.

Question: What strength will you need to open a major suit?

Answer: A five-card suit and at least 12 high-card points, including "some" ace or king—that is, an ace or king in either the trump suit or a side suit.

Question: Here's some reviewing for you—what does "on the board" mean?

Answer: "The board" is another term for the dummy. "On the board" means that, during the play, declarer has won the last trick in dummy, and it is now his or her turn to play a card from dummy, that is, "from the board."

Look at this hand:

♠ 7 6 3 2
♡ A K 10 8
◇ K Q J
♣ 9 4

Question: Would you open the bidding? If so, with what?

Answer: Yes, you would open the bidding. Absolutely. In the homespun terms that we used at the beginning of the book, it looks like a nice hand. It makes you feel good. You have much more than your share. In fact, according to your new method of evaluating the hand, you have 13 high-card points, plus one distributional point, the club doubleton.

But you don't have a five-card major suit. As we have said, if you have sufficient strength, but you do not have a five-card major suit, you open your minor suit. The bid to make here is 1◇, according to the core of our system.

THE MINOR SUIT BORDERLINE

It is time to admit that we have been a little vague, although you may not have noticed it. We have never come right out and said what we meant by "sufficient strength" when we were talking about opening in a minor suit. You certainly have the right to think that we implied that it is the

same as "sufficient strength" when talking about opening in
hearts or spades. But we didn't say that. We must add an
important caution.

You may open with a minor suit that has fewer than five
cards. (In fact, it is required, if you do not have a five-card
major suit or a five-card minor suit.) Look at this hand:

Qxx   Jxx   AQxx   Kxx

No voids, singletons, or doubletons. No distributional values. It is a 12-point hand, period. It does not have that inher-
ent shape value that is present in hands with five-card suits.
You need a little bit more to open.

Here is the final statement of the rule for opening suit
bids:

*You open all hands with a major-suit bid if you have a
five-card major suit, and at least 12 high-card points, including an ace or king.*

*If you do not have a five-card major suit, you open all
hands with 12 high-card points, including an ace or king,
and at least one distributional point, by bidding your minor suit.*

Of course, even if you did not have any distributional
points, you would make your minor-suit bid if you had at
least one extra high-card point.

So, as we said, the bid to make with

♠ 7 6 3 2
♡ A K 10 8
◇ K Q J
♣ 9 4

is 1◇. The hand has more than "sufficient strength": 13 high-
card points, one distributional point, "some ace or king,"
but no five-card major suit.

You may see that we could have made all of the "point
count" portions of the rule much easier for you. We could

have simply told you to open all hands, major or minor, with 12 high-card points and at least one additional distribution or high-card point. We could have given it to you in such a nutshell and saved all of the bother about pointing out that hands with five-card suits always have a short suit. We might have skipped the analysis of cards and hands on the border-line. We might have made it really easy for you and just said: Open any hand with any assortment of 13 points. That'll work most of the time.

That would have seemed easier. But we are certain that many of the issues would have nagged at you without our raising them. When you sit down at the table, you will be glad that you have appreciated these things. The analysis will coalesce, and so will your confidence.

Take a moment now to go back to page 110 and reread the "final statement" of the rule for opening bids. That is a quick summary of the last two chapters. But now, those bones have real flesh on them.

We want you to notice something. More and more, we have been using a lot of bridge vocabulary and making a lot of assumptions about what you now know about the cards. We have not been pointedly teaching these words and ideas. We have been using them as background to explain other things. You are taking in a lot of building blocks!

Question: You are dealer. What would you bid? Count your points. Count them exactly. This is not the time for vainglorious ballparking. Players of bridge count their points. Try not to move your lips when you do so. But better to move your lips than not to count your points:

> ♠ K J 10 8 6 4
> ♡ 9 7
> ◇ Q 10
> ♣ A Q 3

Answer: 1♠.

Question: You are East. North dealt and passed. What would you bid?

♠ A 10 6 4 3 2
♡ K 10
◇ 9 3
♣ Q J 5

Answer: Pass.

Question: You are dealer at South. What would you bid?

♠ 9 8
♡ J 3 2
◇ A Q 6
♣ A J 10 9 7

Answer: 1♣.

Question: South and West pass. You are North. What would you bid?

♠ 3 2
♡ A K 7 6 5
◇ J 5 4
♣ 9 8 7

Answer: Pass.

Question: You are North. You dealt. What would you bid?

♠ K 6 3
♡ K J 6 3
◇ A 10 8
♣ Q J 5

Answer: 1◇.

The rule tells you to bid your longer minor suit, and, if they are equal, your stronger.

You might have a 4–4 fit with South in hearts. She knows that a minor-suit opening describes a hand that does not hold a five-card major suit, but may hold one, or even two, four-card major suits. She knows that your system is always looking for fits in the major suits. She won't be misled. She knows that you may not be intending to find a fit in diamonds.

We have talked about "artificial" bids before. You could say that the 1◇ bid is "artificial." (You do not really want to play the hand in that suit.) It is not a "natural" bid. You would not come to it with your intuition. But, in our system, if you and partner are on the same wavelength, it is absolutely descriptive. Under the rules of the system, any other bid would be confusing. And the meaning of your opening bid will be further clarified by your next bid.

Some people use some very artificial bids. For example, as we told you earlier, "1♣" in one system means that you felt the earth move. As you know, all of these very artificial bids are permitted, as long as you tell your opponents their meaning before you play. In addition, it is a rule of bridge that, after any bid, the next person to bid may turn to the partner of the previous bidder and ask how he or she interprets the bid. You get some amazing and even humorous answers, and some raised and despairing eyebrows from the bidder, when you are playing with a fly-by-the-seat-of-your-pants partnership.

With a fifteen-word vocabulary and only thirty-eight phrases to describe a zillion hands, in a game that was made up by people who love fifty-two funny cards, it is a little difficult to draw a distinction between "artificial" and "natural." In bridge, as in anything, it is good to be, and very often your bids will be, "natural." But sooner or later, to be "natural" would really be misleading. In our system, to open 1♡ with a four-card heart suit would be "unnatural." It would be . . . well . . . weird.

12

BIDDING: OPENING IN NO TRUMP

We have been looking at suit bids. Now look at this hand:

♠ K Q 7 6
♡ A J 3
♦ K 7 2
♣ Q J 10

You have seen this hand before, way back on page 31. These are good cards. Now, you can be more precise when you describe this hand. There is no five-card major suit. The hand has balanced distribution, with 16 high-card points.

Question: How many tricks do you need to make game in a No-Trump contract?
Answer: Nine. If you said "three," you meant "six plus three," and we are still very proud. You really are absorbing this book.

Still, even though you need only nine tricks, making those nine tricks without a trump suit can be more difficult than making ten tricks at spades or hearts. A 4–4 trump fit plays better than 3NT. You will see that when you begin to play. Those trumps just do wonders for you. Therefore, to open in 1NT, you must have a little more high-card strength. And you never count distributional points when you are making a bid in No Trump; short suits are liabilities in No Trump.

Question: Why?

Answer: Your opponents have a lot of them, and you can't trump.

But there is no reason to develop "fear of No Trump," which, we must emphasize, is a malady with no physiological basis whatsoever. No-Trump hands, played without a "power suit," are a great opportunity to learn how to manage your high cards. In many ways, they are easier to keep track of. Your high cards really look like high cards, and, at 3NT, you will have a lot of them. A correctly bid No-Trump contract is very playable, and you should never avoid it if it is the proper contract.

To open in 1NT, you must have 15–17 high-card points, with balanced distribution, and you must have "stoppers" in three suits.

Without trumps, you must be able to control the play of the hand with high cards. You have to be able to "stop" the defenders from winning too many tricks in a suit "from the top," that is, by leading down from the ace to the king and so on. (You sit there with all your high cards, you have reached a 3NT contract with one unstopped suit, and you watch them take five, even six tricks in the unstopped suit, reading each other's signals, transporting unerringly back and forth between their hands as though they had telepathy. They can barely contain their giggles. Oh is that a rueful experience. "Any more?" You finally blurt, as they slowly and slyly slither their diamonds down one by one. "Just . . . one . . . MORE, Mr. Fancy Bidder Man.") An ace will "stop" the opponents from running a suit. So will a king, but only if it is protected. The king is "protected" as long as you hold at least one other card in that suit which can be played if the opponents play the ace. This king has "backup," or a "backer."

All of these holdings are considered "stoppers" in a suit:

A   Kx   Qxx   Jxxx

What do we mean by "balanced distribution"?

4–3–3–3
4–4–3–2
3–3–5–2

Look at the hand we started with once more:

♠ K Q 7 6
♡ A J 3
◇ K 7 2
♣ Q 7 10

The proper opening bid is 1NT. Actually, this hand has stoppers in all the suits.

Question: What would you bid with these hands?:

1. ♠ Q 10 3
   ♡ K 6
   ◇ J 5 4 3
   ♣ A J 8 7

2. ♠ A K 9
   ♡ 9 3 2
   ◇ 10 8 6
   ♣ A Q J 7

3. ♠ A K Q 6
   ♡ A Q J 3
   ◇ 7 5 4
   ♣ 3 2

4. ♠ A K J 6
   ♡ A Q 9 3
   ◇ K 5 4
   ♣ 3 2

Answer: 1. Pass. You don't have enough points for No Trump or a suit bid.

2 1♣. The hand is evenly distributed but doesn't contain enough points or "stoppers" for 1NT.

3. 1◇. It's true that the hand has balanced distribution and 16 high-card points. But look at the three small diamonds and the doubleton club. All of your points are in two suits, a configuration woeful in No Trump.

4. 1NT. The fact that you have a suit that is not stopped should not worry you. This is, after all, a partnership game. In other words, if your partner has a hand that also looks like a No-Trump hand or looks as if it can support a bid in No Trump, he or she will also bid No Trump, and you can count on him or her for a stopper that you don't have.

So, let us state the rule again:

Open hands with 1NT if you have 15–17 high-card points, balanced distribution, and stoppers in three suits.

Look at this North hand:

♠ A J 4
♡ 7 6
◇ A Q 6 3
♣ K Q J 6

This is a 1NT bid.

South, in her turn, bids 3NT. With her hand, over her partner's 1NT bid, her 3NT bid is one of the most precise in all of bridge. (Skipping ahead: 3NT, in response to 1NT, says: "I have at least ten high-card points and an evenly distributed hand. The system promises that our combined hands give us a good play for game in No Trump.") Here are both hands:

North	♠ A J 4
(declarer)	♡ 7 6
	◇ A Q 6 3
	♣ K Q J 6
	♠ Q 6 2
South	♡ A Q J
(dummy)	◇ J 5 2
	♣ 9 8 5 3

The hand is in control. South's hearts supply the missing stopper (actually, stoppers). There are eight sure tricks. There are very good plays for the ninth.

$$♠A, ♠Q \text{ or } ♠J = 2$$
$$♡A, ♡Q \text{ or } ♡J = 2$$
$$◇A, ◇Q \text{ or } ◇J = 2$$
$$♣Q \text{ and } ♣J = 2$$

As for that ninth trick:

If the defenders' clubs "split" favorably, there will be a third trick in clubs.

Question: Can you figure out the possible "splits" that will work for declarer?

Answer:

A10x	xx
Axx	10x
xxx	A10
A10	xxx
xx	A10x
10x	Axx

that is, any 3–2 split.

There are other plays for a ninth trick, or even a tenth trick. For example, there is a play for three tricks in hearts. Let's look at this. This is one of those situations in which to take your time. Read the next paragraph only while checking everything we say against the hands.

The play for three tricks in hearts involves "finessing." We will discuss finessing again but take a preview now. If East holds the ♡K, and if declarer leads hearts "through" her, East will be in a bind. Let's see how it would look:

If declarer leads ♡6 from his hand through East:

(declarer)
- ♠ A J 4
- ♡ 7 *
- ◇ A Q 6 3
- ♣ K Q J 6

"♡6"!

♡ K 10 9 8 ??

(dummy)
- ♠ Q 6 2
- ♡ A Q J
- ◇ J 5 2
- ♣ 9 8 5 3

East is in a bind. If East plays the ♡K, dummy will "cover" with the ♡A, and then the ♡Q and ♡J will be good, for a total of three heart tricks. To see East's dilemma clearly, picture only the heart suit:

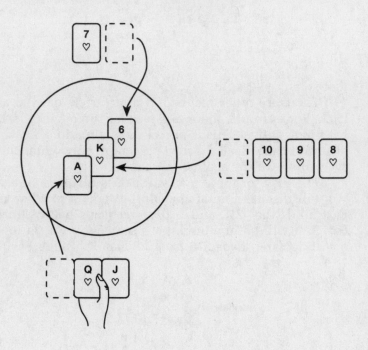

If East doesn't play the ♡K, declarer will "finesse the queen." That is, he will play the ♡Q and win the trick:

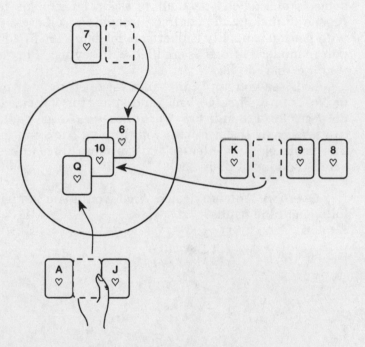

Then declarer will go back to his hand to lead a heart through East a second time. Once again, if East plays the ♡K, he will cover with the ♡A, or, if East "ducks," he will again finesse, and win, with the ♡J. Afterward, the ♡A will be good. In all scenarios, if East holds ♡K, declarer will be able to take three heart tricks.

The play of this hand turns on some "ifs"—if the clubs split in such-and-such a way, if it is East and not West who holds the ♡K. (If West does hold the ♡K, he will beat the ♡Q when declarer first tries the finesse, and declarer will get only two heart winners—♡A and ♡J.) But they are reasonable "ifs." It is well within the universe of possibility to expect to make this hand. Declarer will play the cards "as if" they lay where he wanted them to be. We're not going to show you all four hands this time. Let's leave the defenders' hands in the realm in which they always lie at trick one, subjects of excited speculation, as declarer plans his approach to making his contract. Josephine Culbertson, who, with her husband, Ely Culbertson, made up the first famous pair in modern bridge, is credited with saying, "Play 'em the way they have to lie."

Let's see you apply the rules for opening bids in suits or No Trump. First, go back, and study the italicized rules on pages 90, 110 and 115. Burn these into your brain.

(We know that we have you flipping back and forth in this book. Nothing pleases writers more than to see dog-eared versions of their book.)

Question: You are dealer. What would you bid with the following nine hands?

1. ♠ 10 8
   ♡ Q 6
   ◇ A Q J 10 6 5
   ♣ K J 3

2. ♠ K 10 3
   ♡ A 10 3 2
   ◇ Q 6 5
   ♣ A 10 3

3. ♠ A K 6 5 2
   ♡ 6 5
   ◇ Q 3 2
   ♣ J 10 4

4. ♠ A 6
   ♡ K Q J 5 4
   ◇ K 3 2
   ♣ 7 6 5

5. ♠ 7 6 5 4
   ♡ A Q 7
   ◇ Q J 6
   ♣ A Q 5

6. ♠ 7 4
   ♡ A Q J 7
   ◇ 8 6 2
   ♣ A K Q 9

7. ♠ K 10 6 2
   ♡ A 9 5 4
   ◇ A Q
   ♣ J 6 2

8. ♠ 10 8 6 5 4
   ♡ A K
   ◇ A Q J 10
   ♣ 6 3

9. ♠ K Q 10 9 7
   ♡ A K 10 8 4
   ◇ 6 3
   ♣ A

Answers:
1. 1◇.
2. 1♣.
3. Pass.
4. 1♡.
5. 1NT.
6. 1♣. There is strength and distribution, but there are only two suits with stoppers—not 1NT.
7. 1♣. It is your longer minor suit.
8. 1♠.
9. 1♠. With two five-card majors, always open with spades.

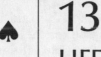

13
LIFE AFTER OPENING

When you respond or rebid (make any second or further bid), you may definitely name a four-card suit. You are invited to do so, even if it is a major suit. And you must not respond or rebid in a suit with fewer than four cards.

RESPONSES AND OVERCALLS: LESS STRENGTH

You need fewer points to *respond* than you need to open.

The reason is this: You already have heard your partner's bid. If partner has sufficient strength to open, even if you have a less than average hand (actually, even with 6 high-card points, if he or she has named a trump suit that you can support), you have a reasonable chance to make a "two bid." And your partner might have a very strong hand, which he or she will make clear by his or her rebid. With six points in support, if you passed, you could be missing a chance for game.

You also need fewer points to *overcall* than you need to open (although you need a few more points than you need to respond). First of all, you want to make the auction competitive. Just because the opponents open the bidding, it doesn't mean that your team can't compete for the contract. Second, an overcall is usually safe. You might get stuck in a difficult contract, but the odds of any deal say that your partner has some values. And, if not, then it looks like your opponents have real strength, and they are not simply going to double your bid. They are looking for bigger fish, and they will bid on.

THE BEACON

It is time to focus upon the direct connection between the number of combined points you and your partner have and whether or not you can make game or slam.

That connection is a beacon. When you respond and overcall, and when you rebid, the system is also designed to explore, along with the search for a trump fit, whether your combined point count can take you to game or slam. When you bid, you are saying, among other things, "I've got so many points. How many have you got?" Or: "My points take me this far. With that, do yours and mine add up to game? To slam?" Sometimes, your first bid will suggest a range of strength, and your next bid will show whether you are in the low or the high portion of that range.

What follows is a crucial piece of the superstructure of bidding strategy.

To make nine tricks at No Trump, or 3 NT, you need 25 or more combined high-card points.

To make ten tricks at ♡ or ♠, or 4♡, 4♠, you need 25 or more combined points.

To make twelve tricks, or a small slam, you need 33 combined points.

To make thirteen tricks, or a grand slam, you need 37 combined points.

There it is. Those four sentences give you your bearings in the auction. Now you know what you are looking for.

Each time the bidding goes up a level, you need a certain amount of additional strength to make the hand. You and your partner share this knowledge of the point levels, and your minds are always seeking point-count data from each other. Before each new bid, you can tally whether you are assured of at least a certain combined total, to judge whether your choice of bid would be responsible.

If you have 14 high-card points, and your partner's bid shows between 6 and 10, you don't have game. That is the way it is. Play at the lowest sensible contract.

Review of game and slam contracts:

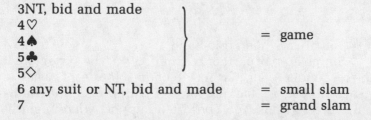

3NT, bid and made
4♡
4♠   } = game
5♣
5◇
6 any suit or NT, bid and made   = small slam
7   = grand slam

Bonuses for game and slam! (See page 219). Therefore, 4♡ bid and made is worth more than 3♡ bid and made. On the other hand, 3♡ bid and made is worth more than 4♡ bid and down. You are looking for game and slam, but you are also limited by the cards that you hold.

As to point count: You need a minimum of 6 high-card points to respond to any opening bid.

To name a new suit at the two level, you need 10 or more high-card points.

Without 10 high-card points, you do not have the luxury of naming new suits and thereby postponing the news that you have a trump fit.

You need 22 combined points to play a suit contract at the three level. You have to keep this reality in mind not only for yourself, but for the position you may create for

your partner, who might go on searching for a fit and take
you to a level where you don't have the strength to make
the contract.

Look at a hand with 16 high-card points. However, before you do, rest assured that the discussion of these next
two hands may be the most "difficult" discussion of the
book. Do not try to memorize this. It is only one of a zillion
possible bidding situations. *Do* follow the logic. The logic
of high-card points is made up of variations on the theme
of simple addition, and respect for bidding levels.

> ♠ K 10 3
> ♡ A Q 10 7
> ◇ A K 4 3 2
> ♣ 9

You always open this hand 1◇.

Suppose your partner responds 1♠? The system invites
the responder (your partner) to name a four-card major suit.
(After all, you are looking for 4–4 trump fits.) But you have
only three spades. You could not support what might be a
four-card spade suit with three spades $(4+3=7=$ not
enough trumps!). Okay. Bid 2♡. The system also invites the
opener to name a four-card major on the second bid.

Notice this: Your partner might be able to support hearts
or diamonds. Your 2♡ bid has offered a choice, and it is a
choice that partner can make only by supporting one or the
other suit by a bid at the three level! No problem. Your 16
high-card points, plus the 6 high-card points guaranteed by
partner's response, give you more than the 22 combined
points your partnership will need to communicate at the
three level. With your strength, in this situation, your 2♡
bid is responsible.

Look at a hand with the same shape, but with 12 high-card points:

♠ K 8 3
♡ K 10 7 2
◇ A Q 4 3 2
♣ 9

You always open this hand with 1◇. The bidding continues. Once again, your partner says 1♠:

S	W	N	E
1◇	Pass	1♠	Pass
?			

Now, what do you bid? Answer: 2◇! This hand has the same distribution as the previous hand, but it has minimum strength. As in the previous hand, your partner has *thus far* guaranteed only 6 high-card points. Therefore, for all you know, the partnership may have only 18 combined high-card points. Your hand is simply not strong enough to show your hearts, which would be to force a choice at the three level.

It would not be responsible, with this strength, to invite your partner to make a choice at the three level. It would be misleading. In this auction, such a bid would really guarantee that you had at least 16 points.

Question: Why is that?

Answer: By forcing a bid at the three level, you would imply—guarantee—that you can add enough points to your partner's guaranteed 6 points to go exploring in three-level territory. (22 − 6 = 16). In the first hand, with 16 points, 2♡ was responsible. Here, with a minimum hand unable to support spades, your only appropriate action is to rebid your diamonds.

Now, it will be up to your partner. Partner may pass and leave it at 2◇ or may bid on. Partner *may* have a big hand and will be letting you know as the auction proceeds. His bid will put the situation into a clearer context and may well encourage you, or even require you, to keep things going.

Therefore, on any bid, you must be sure that your bid level is consistent with combined strength. You also must be sure that you will not force or invite your partner up to a level which exceeds your combined strength. The flip side is: Whenever your bid might send your partner up another level, you should be guaranteeing that you understand that and can contribute the necessary strength to justify bidding at that level. This is the heart of bidding strategy.

Now stop that hand-wringing! The logic of the last two hands, if it were isolated from the game of bridge, would be less demanding than the arithmetic that children use to divide up bags of Halloween candy. It's true. (Assuming, of course, that they have learned to share. Ah well, in bridge, at least, you have to share if you want to win.)

We understand that we are giving you a lot to think about, but rest assured that the system has already been designed to incorporate these realities of point-count levels. We will come back to these hands in Chapter 15. Just make sure now that you definitely understand these two hands and the discussion. Remember, this is the true core of the book. Absorb this discussion, and then press on. *And any bid that does not adjust to these realities does not accurately describe the hand.*

Question: What do these numbers mean to you: 12, 6, 22, 25?
Answer: They are the points needed to open, respond, play at the three level, make game.

Thus, when you respond or rebid, your strategy is:
• Evaluate your hand with point count.
• Your bid should describe your hand.
• You are looking for a fit. With limited strength, if you have a fit, you'd better announce it now.
• You have an objective. You are looking for game, if you can get there. You are looking for slam, if you can get there.

• You don't want to overbid your combined strength or force your partner to make a choice at a level that is above your combined strength.

REEVALUATING YOUR HIGH CARDS

As the bidding continues, your hand exists in a context. You have heard bids, and you have information.

Your doubleton queen (Qx) is strong if your partner bid the suit and weak if an opponent bid the suit.

Your king is weak if your left-hand opponent bid the suit and strong if your right-hand opponent bid the suit. Stop! Be sure that makes sense.

Sit very still, and turn in your mind to your left and then to your right. Imagine yourself, between righty and lefty, your hand close to your vest, your king snuggled in. You hold Kx. Those defenders are on either side of you. How will the cards flow? Where would you like the ace to be, if it can't be in your partner's hand?

Would you like to play your king after the player with the ace decides to play it or not, or would you like it hovering behind you after you play? We probably tipped you off just a little with the word "hovering." Your king is stronger if "righty" holds the ace, (and he or she probably does if he or she bid the suit).

Your evaluation of your hand should have a heavy dose of realism—of your growing awareness of how the cards will play.

REEVALUATING DISTRIBUTION POINTS

You should always evaluate and, on each successive bid, reevaluate your distributional points in the light of whether or not your partner has supported your suit or named a suit that you can support. It is easy to do, since you already have gotten a good sense of your hand when you arranged it and while you listened to the bidding. Basically, until you know that you have a fit, or unless you have significant additional high-card strength, you should not overvalue your distributional values. But *once the auction uncovers a trump fit,* your distributional strength is clarified, and you can increase your short-suit values. Now:

$$\text{Singleton} = 3$$
$$\text{Void} \quad = 5$$

Game level in a suit contract is expressed as 25 total points, not just high-card points. By the time you contract for game, you should have found your trump fit.

Of course, when you name or contract in No Trump, your "points" must all be high-card points.

RESPONSES (AND REBIDS)

The Shape of Your Hand

Pause a moment to review opening-bid suit choices, which we have already asked you to burn in and are sure you have. "Burn in" does not mean that you can spew them like a robot. It means that you are confident that you will play in accordance with them as each situation arises.

The overarching rule is: Open with a five-card major.
Always bid the longer suit first.
With two five-card majors, open the bidding with 1♠.
If you do not have a five-card major, and the minor suits are equal in length, bid the stronger.

Your opening bid will tell your partner a great deal about the shape of your hand. Check us out on this. What follows is simply logic. If you stick to the rules for opening, the opening bid describes the following:

1♣ or 1◇: No five-card major; may have a four-card major; may have four cards in each major

1♡: At least five hearts; could have four spades. Might have six hearts; but then would not have more than five spades.

1♠:   At least five spades; could also have five or
              four hearts. Might have six spades, and then
              could have six hearts, which would be a
              pretty unusual hand.

AKxxx	AKJx	AKxxx	AKxxxx
QJxxx	QJxxx	QJxxxx	QJxxxx
K9	Ax	Ax	———
x	Jx	———	A
Bid 1♠.	*Bid 1♡.*	*Bid 1♡.*	*Bid 1♠.*

The rule works for minor suits as well:

> A
> J
> KQJxx
> Axxxxx
>
> Bid 1♣.

But

> A
> Jxxxx
> A
> Axxxxx
>
> Bid 1♡.

Remember the overarching rule for opening: Identify a
five-card major.

Now let's return to the point of view of the responder.
Watch how nicely it works.

If your partner opens in a major, and you have three of
them, you can support her. You have a 5–3 trump fit! You
know it right off the bat.

If your partner opens in clubs or diamonds, name a
four-card major if you have one. It is not necessary that the

responder have a five-card major suit. The system is seeking four-four trump fits. The system asks the responder to bid a four-card major, if he or she has one. By doing so, if the opener holds a four-card major, the team will have immediately uncovered a 4—4 fit!

Once the bidding has started, all responses in a new suit assure at least a four-card suit. No one can name a new suit without at least four cards in that suit. And the opener can bid a new four-card suit on his or her second bid, even if partner has not previously bid it.

Responder should bid the longer suit first. With two four-card majors, bid hearts. With two five-card majors, bid spades.

Your partner opened 1♣. You hold:

♠ A K 8 7
♡ 7 5 4 2
◇ J 10
♣ 9 8 6

Bid 1♡!

Summary: *Everything you need to know to respond and rebid:*

You need 6 high-card points to respond.

You may name a new suit at the one level. You could have six points. You could have a huge hand. You must have at least 10 high-card points to name a new suit at the two level. It follows that, if you name a new suit at the two level, your partner will understand immediately that the partnership has at least 22 combined high-card points, and that you have not necessarily denied support for his or her suit. You have the "room" to postpone and to clarify, and you will.

You need four cards to name a new suit when you respond or rebid. In fact, you should not hesitate.

You are alert for eight-card trump fits.

Once a trump fit is uncovered, singleton = 3 points, void = 5 points.

Responder may not postpone announcing a fit with fewer than 10 points—support the opener's suit at the two level.

When responding by naming a new suit, bid the longer. With two four-card majors, bid hearts. With two five-card majors, bid spades.

You need 22 points to play at the three level, 25 points for game. You are mindful of these levels. You do not count on strength that has not been guaranteed. You do not guarantee strength that you do not have.

NOW YOU ARE READY TO RESPOND AND TO REBID!

APPLYING WHAT YOU NOW KNOW

Let's look at how the system leads you to eight-card fits and makable contracts. Look at two well-bid hands:

West

♠ Q 10 6 4
♡ A K 7 5
◇ A 3 2
♣ J 10

♠ K J 5 3
♡ Q 9 4
◇ K J 10 9
♣ K 5

East

The bidding:

S	W	N	E
Pass	1◇	Pass	1♠

East responded 1♠. *The system asks the responder to bid a four-card major, if she has one.* In this hand, the system is very definitely going to work out. The partnership will find a very playable 4–4 trump fit. The fit will be in spades. The bidding continues:

S	W	N	E
Pass	1◇	Pass	1♠
Pass	2♠!		

We have found our fit! It would have been wrong for West to use this opportunity to boast about his hearts. By the time of a rebid, you should announce the fit if it has been uncovered. The most important thing for West to do now is to establish that the partnership has a trump fit in spades. You always describe your hand. But once the auction has started, you use your bid to describe what is most relevant about your hand in the light of your partner's bid. You never bid in the abstract. Here East is not misled. She knows that West's opening bid meant that West had high cards lurking somewhere in his hand, and not necessarily in the trump suit. His 2♠ rebid tells East that the partnership can work together.

One of the things that the system uncovers is 4−4 major-suit fits! It surely does!

What should East now bid? The answer is: 4♠! She has opening-bid strength—13 high-card points. Facing her partner's opening bid, her team has at least 25 high-card points. They have found their fit. They have the combined strength to justify bidding game!

We have been stressing major-suit fits, and that is because you have to win only ten tricks to score game in hearts and spades. Our system is designed to be on the lookout for heart and spade fits. However, the system will just as accurately take you to a contract in diamonds or clubs, or in No Trump, if that is where the fit lies.

After an opening bid, the objective is to investigate and to determine, by successive bids:

Is there a major suit fit?

If not, can we play No Trump? During the auction, has your partner bid the suits in which you do not have stoppers? If it develops that you become assured that the combined hands contain enough strength for game, nine tricks with stoppers is easier than eleven tricks with a club or diamond trump suit. (The shape of the two hands does not have to be balanced to play in No Trump!)

If none of the above apply, the bidding will indicate that you have a fit in a minor, and you should not be afraid to

play in it, and even to bid to game in the minor if you have
the combined strength for eleven tricks (28 points).

Look how it all works in this specific situation:

	West (dealer)		**East**
♠ Q J 5 4		♠ A K 8 7	
♡ A J 10		♡ 7 5 4 2	
◇ 10 7		◇ J 5	
♣ A Q 7 3		♣ 9 8 6	

The bidding should be:

West: 1♣. I have no five-card major, but I have sufficient
strength to open.

East: 1♡. I have at least four hearts and at least 6 high-
card points.

West: 1♠. I don't have four hearts, or else I would have
raised to 2♡. I do have exactly four spades.

East: 2♠. I have support for your spades. We have found
our fit. My 1♡ response, I know, from your vantage point,
meant at least 6 points, but perhaps much more. Now I am
making clear that I have a minimum hand. If I had a bigger
hand, with my spade support, I would have jumped to 3♠,
maybe even 4♠, if I were assured of the combined strength
for game. What was your 1♠ bid? Tell me more.

West—Pass. My hand is also in the low range of (opening) strength. We're not going anywhere.

Question: Your partner, West, opens 1♠, and North
passes. What would you bid with these cards?:

♠ 5 3
♡ A Q 7 5 2
◇ 10 7 5
♣ 9 4 2

Be careful. . . .

Answer: 1NT! You can't name your heart suit at the one level because in this auction 1♡ is no longer available. (Your partner has already named spades at the one level, and you must bid up the ladder.) And you don't have enough strength (10 high-card points) to bid a new suit at the two level. You have seen hands like this before. This is another variation of the "saga" on page 50.

Question: Here is a hand with 6 high-card points. After your partner opens 1♠, what do you bid?

♠ Q 10 3
♡ K 6
◇ J 7 6 3
♣ 10 8 6 2

Answer: 2♠—a 5–3 trump fit. With a minimum hand, you must show your support for your partner's suit now.

Question: Here is a hand with 6 high-card points. Partner opened 1◇:

♠ K J 3
♡ 7 6 5 2
◇ Q 10
♣ 9 8 7 4

What is your bid?
Answer: The correct response is 1♡. You are still at the one level. You're always on the lookout for a major-suit fit. Do you have a fit? You don't know yet.

Question: Here is a hand with 6 high-card points. Partner opened 1♣.

♠ K J 3
♡ 7 6 5
◇ Q 10 9 4
♣ 9 8 5

What is your bid?

Answer: The correct response is 1◇. Over 1♣, with 6 or more high-card points and no four-card major, and with four diamonds, 1◇ is available and should be bid. You are naming a new suit, but you are still at the one level.

Your partner opens 1◇. Look at two 10-point hands, both with five-card club suits. With exactly 10 high-card points, you are on the borderline of naming a new suit at the two level. It is a time when you must use your judgment. With exactly 10 high-card points, you need a good five-card suit. (With 11 or more high-card points, you have some leeway, and should follow the general rule of responding with four-card suits.)

♠ K 7 5	♠ Q 10 6
♡ A 9 2	♡ 7 5 2
◇ Q 8	◇ 10 6
♣ J 9 6 4 2	♣ A K J 8 5
Bid 1NT!	Bid 2♣!

More about responding at the two level

A response at the two level, in a new suit, is one of the critical junctures in the bidding. It announces that you have at least 10 points. In fact, in our system, it does even more than that. In our system, it is also a *promise* to your partner that you *will* bid at least once more. It is therefore known as a "forcing" bid. You are forced, by your own decision, *not* to pass when the auction comes around to you for the second time. Therefore, once you respond in a new suit at the two level, your partner, the opener, has been promised that he

will have not just one, but at least two more opportunities
to describe his hand. Your bid tells partner that you have at
least enough combined points (12 + 10 = 22) to bid and play
in a suit contract at the three level, or at 2NT. It says that
you are close to the level of game, and it is a definite explora-
tion of that possibility.

This bid is forcing not only on you but also on your
partner. Your response requires the opener to bid a second
time. (He is not forced to bid a third time but will be given
that opportunity.)

Watch this auction:

West

♠ K 6
♡ A Q 10 8 7
◇ 5 3 2
♣ A Q 10

♠ Q 9 7
♡ K 9 3
◇ A Q 10 6 4
♣ 7 5

East

The bidding:

West: 1♡.

East: 2◇. I have at least 10 points. I want you to know
that now. My high-card strength is more relevant to my response with this holding than announcing a trump fit. Don't
worry, I have enough strength to postpone announcement of
a fit. I may have support for your hearts. You are forced to
bid, and I promise to bid again as well.

West: 2♡. Tell me more.

East: 3♡. Hearts is our suit.

West: 4♡. With your guarantee of 10 points, we have
the combined strength for game.

RULES FOR RESPONDING TO 1NT

Review: To open in 1NT, you must have 15–17 high-
card points, with balanced distribution, and you must have
"stoppers" in three suits.

The rules for responding to 1NT are very precise.

With 0–7 high-card points and a five-card suit or longer,
bid 2◇, 2♡, or 2♠. (Over 1NT, these are "weak bids.")

The reason for requiring a response with weak hands over 1NT is that if the partnership is not going to game (a combined maximum of 24 points), playing in a suit contract with weak hands is safer than playing No Trump. The opener will pass. Look at these North-South hands. Would you rather play them in 1NT or 2◇?:

North

♠ K J 3
♡ J 10 5
◇ K J 8
♣ A Q 7 4

South

♠ 9 8 6 5
♡ 9 6
◇ 10 9 7 5 4
♣ 5 2

A heart lead, which is all too likely, would make you unhappy in No Trump. In 2◇, you can trump the third round of hearts and the hand is playable.

You can't use 2♣ as a weak bid. We use 2♣ over 1NT to show something more important. (With 0–7 points and a club suit, you must pass.)

2♣: *This is an artificial bid, or "convention," known as the Stayman Convention, or "Stayman." It is widely used in response to a 1NT opening bid. With Stayman, you are looking for a fit in a major. Like all No-Trump bidding, it is precise. You must use it if: You have four or more cards in one or both major suits and 8 or more high-card points. You bid 2♣. It asks your partner to name a four-card major suit.* Do not hesitate to check the exact usage—8 or more high-card points (we will be giving you a complete bidding summary) when your partner has opened 1NT and you hold a major suit. It comes up with regularity, it is very useful, and it will probably be "burned in" pretty quickly of its own accord as you begin to play.

Look at this hand:

♠ 7
♡ A J 5 2
◇ Q 6 5 4 2
♣ K 8 7

Your partner has bid 1NT. Bid 2♣. It is a perfect hand for the Stayman convention.

Your bid is forcing. The opener, with no four-card major, must now bid 2◇, but with a four-card major, bids it.

With 8–9 high-card points and no four-card major, bid 2NT (that is, invite the opener to bid 3NT if the 1NT bid was made with a maximum hand).

With 10–15 high-card points and no four-card major, bid 3NT. The bid is precise. Your partner's 1NT bid promised 15–17 high-card points. You need 25 for game. With 10–15 you aren't going to slam, but, with a combined total of 25–30 points, you have a good play for game.

With a five-card major or longer and 10 or more points, bid three of the suit. The bid is forcing. Your partner must bid again. Partner, with three of your suit, will bid game in your major, and without, will bid 3NT.

With both a four-card major and a five-card major and 10 or more points, bid 2♣, and, if partner bids 2◇ (no major), bid three of the five-card suit. The bid is again forcing. Your partner must bid again. With three of your suit, partner will bid game in your major and without, bid 3NT.

Stop now and take a breath. This may seem like much all at once, but if you don't get tense about it, you will see that it fits together and makes sense. None of this is arbitrary. It is no more or less than a tried-and-true code that helps you to match the strength in your hand and your partner's hand with playable bidding levels.

You are learning the codes, the language of bridge! And it will work!

Here are three examples of No-Trump bidding:
West and East are dealt these cards:

	West		East	
♠	7 5 4	♠	Q J 8	
♡	A K 6	♡	Q 7 2	
◇	K J 10 5	◇	6 4 3	
♣	K J 4	♣	A 9 7 6	

The bidding:

West	East
1NT	2NT
Pass (only 24 points, not enough)	

West and East are dealt these cards:

	West		East
♠	A J 8 5	♠	Q 10 6 2
♡	K 6	♡	A Q 9 4
◇	K Q 7 2	◇	J 6
♣	K 9 5	♣	Q 10 3

The bidding:

West	East
1NT	2♣ (Do you have a major?)
2♠ (Yes, spades)	4♠ (Bingo! We have uncovered our fit and we have strength for game)

West and East are dealt these cards:

	West		East
♠	J 10 6	♠	Q 2
♡	A 5	♡	K Q 8 7
◇	K J 9	◇	Q 4 3 2
♣	A K 10 6 5	♣	Q 7 4

The bidding:

West	East
1NT	2♣ (Do you have a major?)
2◇ (No)	3NT

Question: You are responding to a 1NT bid and you hold this hand:

♠ 7 6 2
♡ 10 9 3
◇ A 9
♣ K Q J 7 6

What do you bid? (Take your time. Review the codes if you are not sure.)

Answer: 3NT. Your partner has promised you at least 15 high-card points. You have 10 high-card points—enough for game. (By the way, that strong five-card club suit should third trick ... or ...

OVERCALLS

An "overcall" is a bid made after your opponents have opened the bidding.

To overcall, you always need a good five-card suit and 8 high-card points or more at the one level, 10 high-card points or more at the two level.

These are all good five-card suits:

AQJxx KQ10xx AQxxx KJxxx AJxxx QJ10xx

After your partner overcalls, you should respond the same way you would as if partner had opened the bidding.

LISTENING TO THE BIDDING

One thing may have struck you. If you bid with accuracy, you are describing your hand not only to your partner but to your opponents. And, by the same token, your opponents are describing their hands to you. That is one of the prices that you pay for communicating openly. And it is also one of the ways that you gather information, and one of the challenges and rewards of an open game. You will use what you have learned from the bidding to play and to defend.

Look at this hand. You are West:

♠ 7 6
♡ A 6 3 2
◇ 7 5
♣ 10 8 6 5 4

North-South have the contract at 4♠. The suit was first bid by South.

Question: Who is the declarer? Who is the opening leader?
Answer: South is declarer. West is opening leader.

Question: What should West lead?
Answer: It's difficult to say. He wants to know all of the bidding. Here is the hand again, and the bidding:

♠ 7 6
♡ A 6 3 2
◇ 7 5
♣ 10 8 6 5 4

The bidding:

S	W	N	E
1♠	Pass	2♠	3◇
4♠	Pass	Pass	Pass

East, West's partner, bids diamonds, when North-South had already found their fit and were well on their way to a spade contract. She knew that since South was the first to bid spades, West, her partner, would have the opening lead. East is being very clear. Her strength is in diamonds, and she wants to get 'em while she can. She's using her bid to call for a lead. Lead a diamond.

There are many times when bids help you to spot a card—that is, to tell you whether it is more probably one or the other defender who holds a missing high card. Look at these last four tricks in a No-Trump hand. Declarer, South, has won the last trick. She is in her hand. She needs three of the four tricks to make her contract.

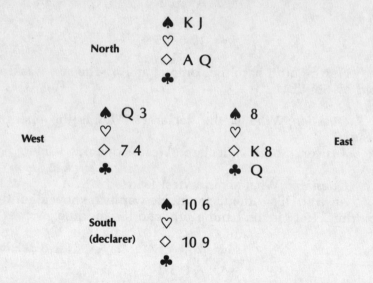

What would you play to win three tricks? It's not easy to say. You have two choices.

You can play a low diamond and hope that West has the ◇K. If he plays low, you will "finesse" the ◇Q and win. If he plays the ◇K, you will cover it with your ◇A, and then the ◇Q will be another winner. The ♠K will give you your third trick . . . or . . .

You can play a low spade and hope that West has the ♠ Q. If he plays low ("ducks"), you will finesse the ♠J and win. If he plays the ♠ Q, you will cover it with your ♠K, and then the ♠J will be another winner. The ◇A will give you your third trick.

You have the chance to try only one of these options. If you were able to look at East's and West's hands you would see that if you try the diamond finesse option, it will lose. East holds the ◇K. You will play your ◇9, West will play low, you will play your ◇Q from dummy with hope in your heart, and your hopes will be smashed. East will win the trick and quickly play her ♣Q for down one.

But you don't know that. It looks like a fifty-fifty chance. Cross your fingers and play a low diamond or a low spade.

But wait, you would know the bidding, of course. You always have to review the bidding in your mind to help yourself play the hand.

This was the bidding:

S	W	N	E
1NT	2♠	2NT	Pass
3NT	Pass	Pass	Pass

Now it's easy. West bid spades. He probably has the ♠ Q. Try the spade finesse. It is entirely reasonable. And, in this hand, you will get your three tricks. The bidding helped you to take your chances from fifty-fifty to almost 100 percent.

Listen to the bidding. During the auction, if you lose track, and it is your turn to bid, you may ask for a review of the bidding. All four players at the table cooperate to reconstruct the bidding with accuracy. Also, during the first trick, when it is your lead or your turn to play a card, you may ask for a review of the bidding.

14

TABLE TALK AND KIBITZING

If you pause now, and let what you have read simmer in your head, you will realize that you now know the game of bridge.

Let us give you a problem. No drawings this time. We'll just use the bridge vocabulary.

Three of your most very favorite people in the world have come over for a game of bridge. You've bought a few nice new decks of cards, and you've gotten out the old card table from the basement. You have a pencil and paper to keep the score, and you and Sally decide that you will square off against Drilla and Bones. You and Sally chat a bit, and you agree that you will use point count, keep on the lookout for major-suit fits, but that you will not open in a major suit unless you have a five-carder.

"What about No Trump?" asks Sally, smiling.

"Fifteen to seventeen," you say. "Even distribution?"

"Of course, even," she says. "Stoppers?"

"Yes, Sally, in at least three suits to open in 1NT."

"How many tricks do we need to bid and make 3NT?" she asks.

"Come on, Sally, you're puttin' me on. That's plastered all over the book."

"I know. So let's play."

You remove the jokers from the deck and put them aside. You draw for high, and you win. You deal, one at a time. You look at your hand. Even distribution: 4–4–3–2. The ♡J, and no other high cards. The doubleton clubs are the ♣2 and the ♣3. It's the worst hand you have seen in a long time. You pass, and so does Bones, who is sitting to your left. Sally bids 1◇. Drilla is arranging her cards and thinking. She starts to say something, but she catches herself. Then she looks at Bones.

"Bones, can I overcall with a real nice heart suit if I have eleven points?"

What, if anything, is going on?

Well, a number of things.

For one, Drilla is doing the unthinkable. She is making "table talk." That is not allowed. Once a hand is dealt, and until the last trick is taken, it's not even permitted to chat about the new neighbor or the score of the ball game. And when someone talks about her hand, it is time to throw the cards up into the air. Bid. Just bid and play. No table talk.

Let's go on. The doorbell rings and it is Aunt Bella. She loves bridge and asks if she can kibitz. "I'll just sit in one spot and look at only one hand and not move around and not say a word."

That's a good kibitzer.

You deal a new hand and start over. Maybe Bella has brought you luck. Look at this hand:

♠ A K J 9 7 3
♡ A K
◇ K Q 10
♣ A 4

Will you open? You will open with your heart on fire. What a spade suit! If Sally has gotten some good cards at the same time you have, you are looking at a possible slam.

Maybe, maybe, a grand slam. Look at those spades. If Sally
has spades . . .

What is going on here?

Well, a number of things.

In the first place you have an incredible hand. Under
our rule, so far, you should open 1♠. But you wonder if
there is some way to communicate to Sally that you have
more than an opening bid. Much more. We have not yet told
you how to open with BIG hands. But just use what you
already have learned. Do you think you can come up with
a bid that describes your hand to Sally? How about opening
with 2♠? That will alert her.

In the second place, you have just read several pages of
a story about bridge, and nobody had to explain to you what
was going on. It rolled into your head so easily—you have
absorbed a great deal. And you now know about table talk
and kibitzing.

15
BIDDING QUIZZES

This chapter is especially quiz-oriented. You will be applying what you already know, and everything will be coming together. Feel free, if you want to check, to look at the bidding summary on pages 174–75, but first try to figure these out without it. Then look at our answers at the end of the chapter.

Question 1: East, your partner, has opened 1♣. South passes. You, West, hold:

♠ J 7 4 3
♡ A K 9
◇ 3
♣ 10 8 6 3 2

What would you bid?

Question 2: Righty opens with 1♡. Would you overcall with this hand?

♠ K 6
♡ Q 5
◇ K Q 7 6 4 3
♣ A 9 8

Question 3: Your partner opens with 1♡. Righty passes. You hold:

♠ 3 2
♡ K 10 9
◇ K 6 5 2
♣ 10 8 3 2

What would you bid?

Question 4: You deal yourself:

♠ A 8
♡ K 6
◇ K J 10 7 2
♣ A K 8 4

What would you bid?

Question 5: North opens 1♡. You are East. What would you bid with these cards?

♠ Q 7 6 4 3 2
♡ 10 9
◇ J 6
♣ Q 8 5

Question 6: West, your partner, opens 1♡, and North passes. You hold:

♠ K 10 8
♡ 7 5
◇ Q 4 2
♣ J 10 7 5 4

What would you bid?

Question 7: West, your partner, opens 1♣ and North passes. You hold:

♠ J 6
♡ K Q J 9
◇ 10 6 2
♣ K 8 6 3

What do you bid?

Question 8: You deal yourself:

♠ Q 10 8 7 4
♡ A K 9 3 2
◇ K J
♣ A

What would you bid?

Question 9: Your partner opens 1♣, righty passes, and you hold:

♠ A Q 5
♡ 7 6 4
◇ 9 8
♣ J 8 7 6 4

What would you bid?

Question 10: Lefty deals and passes, your partner bids
1♡, righty passes, and you hold:

> ♠ A J 6 4 2
> ♡ Q 8
> ◇ 9 8 7
> ♣ K J 5

What do you bid?

Question 11: Your partner opens 1♡, righty passes, and
you hold:

> ♠ 9 5
> ♡ A Q 8 7
> ◇ K 9 7
> ♣ Q 9 4 2

What do you bid?

Question 12: Your partner opens 1♠, righty passes, and
you hold:

> ♠ 10 9
> ♡ A Q 8
> ◇ J 9 7 6 3
> ♣ K 5 2

What do you bid?

Question 13: Lefty deals and passes, your partner bids
1♡, righty passes, and you hold:

> ♠ J 6
> ♡ Q 8 4
> ◇ J 9 7
> ♣ 8 6 4 3 2

What do you bid?

Question 14: Your partner deals and opens with 1♡, righty passes, and you hold:

> ♠ K 9
> ♡ Q 6 3
> ◇ 10 9 8 6
> ♣ J 8 6 4

What would you bid?

Question 15: Your partner opens 1♣, righty passes, and you hold:

> ♠ J 8 5 3
> ♡ A 7 6 4
> ◇ 9 8
> ♣ Q 8 7

What is your response?

Question 16: Your partner opens 1♣, righty passes, and you hold:

> ♠ J 8 5 3 2
> ♡ A 7 6 4
> ◇ 9
> ♣ Q 8 7

What is your response?

Question 17: You deal. These are your cards:

♠ K 7 5 4 2
♡ A 6
◇ A J 3
♣ 9 7 5

What will you bid?

Question 18: Pass, pass, your turn. These are your cards:

♠ Q J 8 7 4
♡ Q J 8
◇ Q J
♣ Q J 6

What is your bid?

Question 19: North dealt and passed. You are East. You hold:

♠ K J 3
♡ A Q J 8
◇ 10 4
♣ A J 9 7

What is your bid?

Question 20: You are South. Your partner, North, opens 1♣. East passes. You hold:

♠ J 10 7 4 3
♡ Q 9 8
◇ 8 4 3
♣ K 10

What do you bid?

Question 21:

W	N	E (you)
1NT	Pass	?

You hold:

      ♠ K 6 3
      ♡ Q 10 8
      ◇ A J 7 3 2
      ♣ 9 7

What would you bid?

Question 22: You, West, hold:

      ♠ J 5
      ♡ A Q 6 4
      ◇ K 8 7 5
      ♣ A 10 9

The bidding is:

W	N	E	S
1◇	Pass	1NT	Pass
?			

What is your bid?

Question 23: You, East, dealt. You hold:

      ♠ K J 3 2
      ♡ K 10 7
      ◇ A Q 4 3 2
      ♣ 9

What would you bid?

Question 24: The bidding continues:

E	N	W	S
1◇	Pass	1♠	Pass
?			

What would you bid now?

Question 25: Suppose we make a change in your (East's) hand:

♠ K J 3 2
♡ K 10 7
◇ A K Q 4 3
♣ 9

How would you open?

Question 26: Once again, the bidding continues:

E	N	W	S
1◇	Pass	1♠	Pass
?			

Now what do you bid?

Question 27: You are East, and you are first bidder. You open 1NT. The bidding is:

E	S	W	N
1NT	Pass	2NT	Pass
?			

This is your hand:

♠ A 8 4
♡ K J 8 3
◇ K Q 10
♣ Q 5 3

What is your second bid?

Question 28: You are West and open 1♡. This is your hand:

♠ K 9
♡ A J 7 6 4 2
◇ Q 10
♣ K 8 2

The bidding:

W	N	E	S
1♡	Pass	2◇	Pass

What is your next bid?

Question 29: You are East. Your partner, West, opens 1♡. North passes. This is your hand:

♠ K 10 9
♡ 4 2
◇ A Q J 10 4
♣ Q 7 5

What would you bid?

Question 30: What is your second bid?

Question 31: You are South. The bidding is:

N	E	S	W
1♠	Pass	?	

What is your bid with this hand?

> ♠ Q 4
> ♡ Q 7
> ◇ K J 10 8 5 3
> ♣ J 9 4

Answer 1: 1♠ is the proper response. You have 8 high-card points, and our system requires a response in a major, and not a raise in clubs. Don't be alarmed if you got this wrong. (Darn!) We have been pouring a lot into you. Loosen up.

Answer 2: Yes. 2◇.

Answer 3: 2♡. You have 6 high-card points. You have at least a 5–3 trump fit. Your response supports your partner at the two level.

Answer 4: 1◇.

Answer 5: Pass. You have insufficient high-card strength to overcall.

Answer 6: 1NT. You have 6 high-card points, the minimum required for a response. You do not have support in your partner's suit. Bid 1NT.

Answer 7: 1♡. You'll find out on your partner's next bid if you have a 4–4 heart fit.

Answer 8: 1♠. With a five-card heart suit, and a five-card spade suit, open with spades.

Answer 9: 2♣.

Answer 10: 1♠. At the one level, a new suit promises at least 6 points, maybe many more.

Answer 11: 2◇. The bid is forcing. It is true that you have uncovered a magnificent trump fit of at least nine cards. But the hand is too strong for a bid of 2♡. You will announce your fit as the auction continues. (The hand is just shy of the strength to jump to 3♡. We will be giving you an inventory of special bids, for bidding bigger hands, in the next chapter.)

Answer 12: 1NT. With exactly 10 high-card points, the hand is just below the borderline of responding with a new suit at the two level; the diamond suit isn't good enough.

Answer 13: Pass. You don't have 6 high-card points.

Answer 14: 2♡. Your partner's 1♡ bid guaranteed at least five hearts. You have found your eight-card trump fit. With 6 high-card points, you don't have the strength to postpone announcing your fit or to make another, stronger, bid.

Answer 15: 1♡. With two four-card majors, bid 1♡. Appreciate how nicely it works. Your partner, if she has four spades, can still bid them at the one level.

Answer 16: 1♠. Responding with a five-card major and a four-card major, name the longer. (With five spades and five hearts, name spades.)

Answer 17: 1♠. It is the perfect opening bid, according to the core of our system.

Answer 18: Pass. You have 12 high-card points (and one distribution point in the doubleton), but you have no ace or king. You don't have enough to open. Suppose the fourth bidder passes? The hand will be "passed out." It happens. Reshuffle and redeal.

Answer 19: 1NT. Absolutely. There is no other bid for this hand. You have 16 high-card points and balanced distribution. Balanced distribution and 15–17 high-card points calls for an opening bid of 1NT.

Answer 20: 1♠. You have 6 high-card points and the requisite four-card major suit. Actually, you have a five-card major suit.

Answer 21: 3NT. You do not hold a four-card major suit. It is not the time to bid 2♣ ("Stayman"). With your 10 high-card points and your partner's guarantee of 15–17 high-card points, you know that you have at least the combined 25 high-card points to bid to game in No Trump, and you should do so.

Answer 22: Pass. Very good bid. Your partner does not have a major and has 10 points at the most. You are not going anywhere. You have nothing more to say about your hand. That describes it.

Answer 23: 1◇.

Answer 24: 2♠.

Answer 25: 1◇. Still no change.

Answer 26: 3♠! This is a "jump raise." When you have opened, and your partner's response tells you that you have a fit, with extra values you should "jump raise." (With the upper range of extra values, you would have "double jump raised" to 4♠.) We will give you the exact point count requirements for "jumps" in the next chapter, "Special Bids."

Answer 27: Pass.

Answer 28: 2♡. There is no more appropriate action here than to rebid your six-card heart suit and await partner's next call.

Answer 29: 2◇. With this many high-card points (in fact, you have the strength of an opening bid in your own hand), you can and should show your strength by naming a new suit at the two level. Diamonds is your suit.

Here is a recap of the bidding:

W	N	E	S
1♡	Pass	2◇	Pass
2NT	Pass	?	

Answer 30: 3NT. An opening bid opposite an opening bid compels you to bid game. Here, with no fit for your partner's hearts and with your spade and club stoppers, 3NT should be the best spot.

Answer 31: 1NT. Not 2◇. You need 10 high-card points to respond in a new suit at the two level.

If you have answered these questions correctly, or if you have understood the answers we have provided, then you have come a long way indeed, a very long way. When you sit down with real people and real cards, don't forget that you know what you are doing.

16
SPECIAL BIDS

We have a few more special bids that we want to tell you about.

BIDDING BIGGER HANDS

Stronger hands invite stronger bids. A strong array of high cards gives realistic value to voids, singletons, and doubletons. In our system, distribution points are definitely relevant when you are considering a bid that will broadcast a stronger hand.

Notice that you should see your hand in one of these categories:

12–15 points: minimum opening bid

16–21 points: extra values

19 or more points: BIG hand

We know that these categories overlap. Use them to help you get a sense of your hand. The actual decisions—to open with a "two bid," to "jump," to "jump shift"—will be made with precision of communication in mind. Don't hesitate to consult this chapter or the bidding summary card for the exact usage—that is, the precise point-count requirements for these bids.

It is a good time to remember that all vocabulary in all languages has meaning only in context. "Fire" can mean the feeling of new love or a warning to get out of the theater. "Two hearts" might mean 6 points (response in support of partner's one-heart opener), zero points ("weak" bid over 1NT), 10 points (response at the two level, naming a new suit), or definitely a monster (opening "two level" bid.) The context makes it clear.

Review: As to A, Ax, and Kx, count both the high-card points and the distribution points.

$$A = 6 \text{ total points}$$
$$Ax = 5$$
$$Kx = 4$$

Once a trump fit is uncovered, the short suits in your hand gain value.

$$Singleton = 3$$
$$Void = 5$$

Jumps

Jumps are clear ways to describe strength in responses and rebids. These bids are precise and are designed for useful application.

Learn some new vocabulary:

Opening bid	Response	Rebid	
1♡	2♠!		= *jump shift* (change suit and skip a level)
1♣	1◇	2♠!	= *jump shift*
1♡	3♡!		= *jump raise*
1♣	1♡	3♡!	= *jump raise*
1♣	1♡	4♡!	= *double jump raise*
1♠	2♣	3♠!	= *jump bid* (skip a level, in the suit you previously bid)

Jumps are part of bridge language. If a jump makes sense (if it describes your hand), and if it is available, use it. Jumps are part of your inventory—your arsenal—of bids.

Jumps by responder:

A jump raise by responder of opener's suit shows 12 or more high-card points and support in the partner's suit. It is forcing to game—it tells the opener that you also have the strength of an opening bid.

A jump shift by responder shows 17 or more high-card points and that responder's suit is a good five-card or longer suit. You are thinking about slam. You already know that together you have at least 29 points between you. With this strength, you can surely postpone announcing a fit, even if you have support for the opener's suit.

Jumps by opener on rebid:

A jump bid shows 16–17 points and a long suit (at least six cards).

After opening one in a suit, a jump to 2NT shows 18–19 points and balanced distribution.

After opening one in a suit, a jump shift shows 18–20 points and unbalanced distribution.

Jumps by opener showing support of the suit bid by his or her partner in a response:

With 16–18 points, jump raise in partner's suit.

With 19–21 points, double jump raise to game.

Consider: If you open with 19 or more points, any response by your partner guarantees game, since partner needs at least 6 points to respond.

Opening at the Two Level and Beyond

With BIG power, say so. Open at the two level. These bids are precise. With:

20–22 high-card points, even distribution = open 2NT

23–24 high-card points, even distribution = open 2♣ *and rebid 2NT*

25 + high-card points, even distribution = open 3NT

22 + points, unbalanced distribution = open 2 of suit

(Note: "2♣" means either 23–24 even, or 22+ with clubs, to be clarified on rebid.)

With these bids, you certainly have your eye on game. Maybe slam.

Conventions

"Artificial" bids that have been designed for very specific situations are called "conventions." Three of these are universally used and fit right into our system. They all ask your partner to give you very specific information about his hand. These are named after their inventors: Mr. Stayman, Mr. Gerber, and Mr. Blackwood.

Stayman: 2♣ over 1NT (see page 141).

Conventions for Slam Bidding:

There are two conventions that are commonly used to investigate the possibility of slam. Both of them ask your partner how many aces he has. They are known as the Gerber and Blackwood conventions; both of them ask: "Do we have enough aces for slam, partner?"

Let's suppose that your partner has opened 1NT, and you hold this hand:

♠ A J 5
♡ K 10
◇ A Q 10
♣ Q J 10 5 3

Since your partner has opened 1NT, you know that there is a real possibility for slam. You have 17 points, and your partner's bid promises at least 15. But your partner could have 15 high card points and yet have no aces. You can't make a slam if your opponents have two aces to cash. Your partner's 1NT opener might look like this:

♠ K Q 10
♡ Q J 9 3
◇ K J 6 4
♣ K 9

You are not really interested in more point-count information. You want to know, specifically, if your partner has any aces. If your partner has one, and since you have two, you know that you have one loser. That's okay. You still can take 12 tricks for a small slam. If partner has none, you know that defenders have the ♡A and the ♣A, and you will be off two tricks. In that case, you don't want to bid to the six level.

Is there a way to ask your partner how many aces she has?

Yes!

The Gerber convention: *Bid "4♣" over 1NT:*

This convention is designed specifically for when your partner has opened 1NT or 2NT, and you, too, have a big hand. Once you respond with 4♣, your partner's next bid must tell you the number of aces he holds:

4◇ = 0 aces or four aces
4♡ = 1 ace
4♠ = 2 aces
4NT = 3 aces

Notice that 4◇ means both 0 or 4 aces. You will always know which is meant by looking at the number of aces in your own hand.

Notice also that the convention has not taken you too

high. If you see that you have insufficient aces, you can simply bid 4NT next and play at that level.

Suppose your partner tells you that he has all the aces you're looking for. You may now want to know about partner's kings. If so, "5♣" asks for kings, and partner will use the same code, at the five level, to tell you the number of kings he holds.

Gerber is an easy and effective convention. When the time comes, don't hesitate to use it. If you get the information you're hoping for, bid your slam.

Gerber is also a difficult convention to miss; "4♣" out of nowhere gets everybody's attention.

The *Blackwood* convention—4NT—is identical in concept to Gerber, but it asks for aces over a suit bid. You begin the inquiry by bidding 4NT. For example:

E	S	W	N
Pass	1♠	Pass	3♠ (a jump)
Pass	4NT!		

North will respond as follows:

$$5♣ = 0 \text{ or } 4 \text{ aces}$$
$$5♢ = 1 \text{ ace}$$
$$5♡ = 2 \text{ aces}$$
$$5♠ = 3 \text{ aces}$$

South can ask for kings with "5NT," and North will use the same code.

PREEMPTS

A *preemptive bid*, or "preempt," is a defensive opening bid, used when you have a weak hand and a long suit. It is designed to make the other team's bidding more difficult by preempting the bidding levels. It can suggest a possible sacrifice. The requirements are specific: a seven-card suit, and 5 to 9 high-card points. It is a good bid. Use it when the cards call for it. You bid three of your suit.

Here is typical "preempt":

♠ 7
♡ J 3
◇ K Q J 8 7 4 2
♣ 9 5 2

Open 3◇.

DOUBLES

We shall now present one last peg in the system: "doubling."

A *double* inflates the potential score of the immediately preceding bid. If the hand is made, the offensive score is multiplied. If the hand goes down, the defensive score is multiplied. (If someone bids after the double—if the double is not "passed out"—the double is wiped out.)

Doubles and redoubles are, technically, "business" or "penalty" doubles and redoubles. These bids mean, "You can't make it," or "Oh yes we can."

"Penalty doubles" are usually bid when the auction has progressed—usually after your opponents' final bid.

Takeout doubles

However, directly after the opening bid, a double is used in place of an overcall, not as a penalty double but as a code to describe your hand. This bid is informational. It informs your partner that you have approximately opening-bid strength, and that you have support in the other suits, that is, in the suits that the opener did not bid. It asks your partner to bid his or her best suit when it is his or her turn to bid. This is called a "takeout double."

Question: South has just bid 1♡. You are in the "second seat" (West), holding these cards:

♠ K Q 7 4
♡ 3
◇ A Q 10 7
♣ K J 6 5

What might be a good bid?

Answer: Double. It is a takeout double. It is the perfect bid. Look at your hand. You have opening-bid strength. You don't really want the double to stand. You want your partner to "take you out" of the double by bidding her best suit. It is a very economical way to say, "I have an opening bid too." It tells your partner about your strength and that you have support in the unbid suits. It asks her to bid.

If North doesn't bid, your partner must bid, even with no points. There is one exception. If your partner is sure that the opener will not make the contract, she can let the double stand.

A redouble that immediately follows a takeout double is also intended as a code. It means "I have 10 or more high-card points." It tells your partner: "It's our hand."

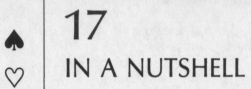

17
IN A NUTSHELL

You have now been confronted with a group of codes for the auction. In the earlier chapters, you learned virtually everything without memorization because it all appealed to your common sense. Now, many of these new codes and point-count specificities might sound confusingly similar— so many points to bid this, just a few more to bid that. You might have a temptation to throw away what you have learned conceptually in a effort to get these rules straight. That is one of the great mistakes of beginning bridge players.

We don't want you to spend your time memorizing anything that we haven't told you to memorize. We suggest that you have a "cheat sheet" to consult while bidding. A summary box of information that we've prepared follows on pages 174–75. You may want to consider tearing it out of the book, photocopying it, or copying it onto an index card. As you play, you'll find that eventually you'll start to memorize a lot of the material. The system weaves together and makes sense.

In our overwhelming concern that you not regard the game of bridge as a challenge of memory but rather as a game that uses general rules and codes to organize the enjoyment, we are going to discharge what may be your need to memorize by isolating four "rocks of knowledge." These are crucial. There is a good chance that you already have emblazoned these principles on your brain. In fact, we previously asked you to memorize the game contracts (3NT, 4♡, 4♠, 5♣, 5◇), which must truly seem like old material by now. We have also asked you to "burn in" the rules for sufficient strength for opening in suits and in No Trump, as well as the rules for opening-bid suit choices. They are in there. No need even to check.

These rocks of knowledge will always serve to orient you, and are well worth memorizing:

1. *In order to make game in 3NT, 4♡, or 4♠, a partnership needs 25 or more points. In 3NT, they must be HCP.*

In order to make a small slam, a partnership needs 33 or more high-card points.

In order to make a grand slam, a partnership needs 37 or more high-card points.

2. *Open all hands with a five-card major suit + 12 high-card points + some ace or king by bidding your suit. With two majors of five or more cards, bid the longer. If they are equal in length, bid spades.*

3. *Open all hands without a five-card major suit but with 12 high-card points including some ace or king plus at least one distribution point by bidding your longer minor suit, or, if they are equal in length, the stronger.*

4. *In order to respond by naming a new suit at the two level, you need 10 or more high-card points. With exactly 10 points, you need a good five-card suit.*

Have you got them? Are they in there with the name of the first president and the guy that hit all the home runs? You must let bridge have a piece of your brain. You have plenty of room. Think of what is already in there that doesn't seem to hurt you.

BIDDING SUMMARY CARD

Opening bids:
  5-card major suit + 12 HCP + some A or K = open 1 of suit.
  No 5-card major suit + 12HCP + some A or K + 1 distributional
  point = open longer, or, if equal length, stronger minor.
      Open with longer suit. Overarching rule: open with 5-
      card major. If 5♡ and 5♠, name ♠.
  Balanced distribution + 15–17 HCP + stoppers in 3 suits = Open
  1NT.
  7-or-more-card suit + 5–9 HCP = open 3 of suit (preemptive bid).
Overcalls:
  With 5-card "good suit," e.g., AQxxx, AJxxx
                                  KJxxx, QJ10xx
  8–10 HCP = bid suit if bid available at 1 level.
  10 + HCP = may bid suit at 2 level.
"Double" (takeout double): Approximately an opening bid
                                  + support for all unbid suits
Responses to your partner's suit bid:
  At least 6 HCP to respond
      Bid 4-card or longer major. (After 1♣, with no
          4-card major, and 4 diamonds, bid 1◇.)
      Respond with longer suit.
      Two 4-card majors = name hearts.
      Two 5-card majors = name spades.
  6–10 HCP + support in partner's suit = raise partner.
  6–10 HCP + no suit to bid at one level = bid 1NT.
  10 or more HCP = may bid new suit at 2 level (with exactly
      10 HCP, bid at 2 level only with a good 5-card suit).
  10 or more HCP over a takeout double = redouble.
  12 or more points + support in partner's suit = jump raise.
  17 or more points + good 5-card suit = jump shift.
Responses to your partner's 1NT bid:
  0–7 HCP + 5 card suit = bid 2◇, 2♡, or 2♠.
  8–9 HCP + no 4-card major suit = bid 2NT.
  8 or more HCP + 4-card major suit = bid 2♣ ("Stayman").
  10–15 HCP and no 4-card major = bid 3NT.
  10 or more HCP + 5-card major + 4-card major = bid 2♣
      ("Stayman"); if partner bids 2◇, bid 3 of 5-card suit.
  10 or more HCP + 5-card major = bid 3 of suit.
Rebids by opener:

Invited to name a 4-card suit, emphasis on major-suit fit.

With support in partner's suit:

> 12–15 points = raise partner.
>
> 16–18 points = jump raise.
>
> 19–21 points = double jump.

Jump bid (jump in opener's suit) = 16–17 points and a long suit (at least six cards).

After opening 1 in a suit, jump to 2NT = 18–19 points and even distribution.

After opening 1 in a suit, jump shift = 18–20 points and unbalanced distribution.

Big opening bids:

> 20–22 HCP, even distribution   = open 2NT.
>
> 23–24 HCP, even distribution = open 2♣ and rebid 2NT.
>
> 25 + HCP, even distribution   = open 3NT.
>
> 22 + points, unbalanced distribution = open 2 of suit.
>
> (*Note:* "2♣" means either 23–24 even or 22 + with clubs, to be clarified on rebid.)

Slam Conventions:

> Gerber: 4♣ over 1NT, asking for aces
>
> Blackwood: 4NT over suit bid, asking for aces

Game = 3NT, 4♡, 4♠, 5♣, 5◇

HCP needed to make 3 NT	= 25
Point count needed to make 4♡, 4♠	= 25
Point count needed to make 5♣, 5◇	= 28
Point count needed to make small slam	= 33
Point count needed to make grand slam	= 37

Question: Who was that guy in the fourth or fifth century who was involved with hordes and terror and swept over the land?

Answer: Attila. Right. He was in there. In your very own brain. And it didn't hurt you. We just don't think that there is a very viable argument that knowing—to the end of your days—that you do not name a new suit at the two level without 10 or more points is anything to fear.

Memorize the four rocks of knowledge. Around them the other rules will cluster and take their rightful place. The rocks will let you memorize the rest of the rules, and turn them into rocks as well.

Shall we test you on these? Not necessary? How about one question?

Question: How many combined points do you need to make 4◇?

Answer: 25, of course. It is a bid to make ten tricks, the same as any other four bid. You need the strength of 25 points to take ten tricks in any suit contract. (But you also know that game in diamonds or clubs is "five"—eleven tricks. For eleven tricks, you'd better have 28 or more points between you and your partner. We did not make this a rock of knowledge since we oriented our "rocks" to the practical goals of bidding game contracts in No Trump and in the major suits.)

"Memorize" is a relative term. Everything that you learn is "memorized." You have already "memorized" a great deal of this book. But it is the case that certain specific things need extra effort at first to keep them straight. It is very important that you keep straight the point-count requirements of game contracts.

Remember, however, and we now use the word "remember" in its conversational sense, that these point-count levels, and all of the other point-count requirements that we have not asked you to memorize, are not arbitrary. They are designed to make sense and to describe your hand. They were not created by people who just threw out numbers. They were created by people who noticed that certain numbers led to certain contracts and that attention to these numbers kept them out of trouble.

For example, as you now well know, you don't need the same strength to respond as you need to open, because bridge is a partnership game. If your partner has the strength to get the ball rolling, then you don't need as much strength to keep the ball in motion. All of the point requirements of all of the bids reflect sensible considerations and try to do so with accuracy.

Drill: For these questions, get an answer in your mind without the use of the summary card, and then look at the card before you look at our answers at the end of this chapter.

Drill 1: North deals and passes. You are East, holding:

♠ 7 6
♡ 3 2
◇ 9 8 7 6
♣ A Q 9 7 4

What is your bid?

Drill 2: You are East. The bidding has been:

W	N	E	S
1NT	Pass		

What would you bid, holding:

♠ K Q 7
♡ A 6 2
◇ K 3
♣ K Q J 6 3

Drill 3: Your partner opens 1♠, righty passes, and you hold:

♠ Q 10 9 7
♡ A J 3
◇ 7 2
♣ K Q J 2

What do you bid?

Drill 4: Dealer opens 1♡ and it's your turn next to bid. You hold:

> ♠ K J 10 9
> ♡ 8 2
> ◇ A Q 8 3
> ♣ Q 10 4

What is your bid?

Drill 5: You are South. Your partner opens the bidding with 1NT, East passes, and this is your hand:

> ♠ K J 3 2
> ♡ A J 7 5
> ◇ Q 4
> ♣ 6 3 2

What will you bid? (It will make us feel very warm and proud if you get this one.)

Drill 6: You are dealer. What would you bid with this hand?

> ♠ 2
> ♡ K J 10 7 6 4 3
> ◇ Q 3 2
> ♣ 10 8

Drill 7: You are North. Here is the bidding:

W	N	E	S
1♠	?		

These are your cards:

> ♠ 7 3
> ♡ K 10
> ◇ A J 10 9 7 4
> ♣ K 9 5

What do you bid?

Drill 8: Your partner, West, opens 1♠, and North passes. What will you bid with these cards?:

> ♠ 5 3
> ♡ A Q 7 5
> ◇ 10 7 4 5
> ♣ 9 4 2

Drill 9: North opens with 1◇, and you, East, are in the second seat. You hold these cards:

> ♠ A Q 9 2
> ♡ K J 3 2
> ◇ 6
> ♣ K 10 8 7

What is your bid?

Drill 10: You are East. The bidding has been:

S	W	N	E
1♠	Pass	2♣	?

You hold:

> ♠ A 10 8 5
> ♡ A 6
> ◇ A K 3
> ♣ J 8 6 4

What would you bid?

Drill 11: In that same hand, North bid to game at 4♠. Now what would you bid? Try to first come up with your answer without looking back at the hand.

Drill 12: You are South. The bidding was:

N	E	S	W
1♡	Pass	3♡	Pass
4NT	Pass	?	

Here are your cards:

> ♠ 10 9
> ♡ Q 7 6 5
> ◇ A 3 2
> ♣ A K J 5

What do you bid?

Drill 13: You open this hand with 1◇:

> ♠ K 10 3
> ♡ A Q 10 7
> ◇ A K 4 3 2
> ♣ 9

Your partner responds 1♠. What is your rebid? Bear a few things in mind. You have seen this hand before, on page

128. We can now discuss your choice more precisely. Your partner has at least six points, maybe no more, maybe many more. You have 16 high-card points. But you can't jump raise, because you can't support his spades. (His response promised only four of them.) A jump raise is a great way to show extra strength and would have been the perfect bid if your partner had responded 1♡. But a jump raise is just not available to you in this auction. And you cannot jump shift (3♡). You don't have enough points.

What do you bid?

Drill 14: We also looked at a hand with the same shape, but with 12 high-card points:

> ♠ K 8 3
> ♡ K 10 7 2
> ◇ A Q 4 3 2
> ♣ 9

Again, you open with 1◇. The bidding continues. Once again, your partner says, "1♠."

S	W	N	E
1◇	Pass	1♠	Pass
?			

Drill 15: Here's one last bidding question. Now get it right. It's nice to go out battered but proud. Count those points. Check that bidding summary. Your partner, North, opens 1♣, and East passes. It's your turn. How would you respond, holding:

> ♠ A Q
> ♡ K Q J 5 3 2
> ◇ K Q J 8
> ♣ 6

How did you do? It would be very helpful for you to go through these questions again, until you get them all right. These questions give you a very valuable review.

Answer 1: Pass.

Answer 2: 4♣ ("Gerber," asking for aces). You have a lot of strength between you. You are going for the marbles.

Answer 3: 3♠, a jump raise.

Answer 4: Double. That is your takeout double. You have described an opening bid, and you are asking your partner to bid her best suit.

Answer 5: 2♣. Perfect! That's the "Stayman" convention. Your partner should name his best four-card major, if he has one, and if not, he will bid 2◇. This is not the time to bid 3NT, even though you have the combined points for it. Trump contracts usually play better than No-Trump contracts, and Stayman is the bid designed to seek game at 4♡ or 4♠ by describing a hand with 8 or more high-card points and one or two four-card majors.

Answer 6: 3♡. That's a preemptive bid, for which you have a perfect hand.

Answer 7: 2◇—an overcall.

Answer 8: 1NT. Another variation of the "saga."

Answer 9: Double. It's a flawless takeout double.

Answer 10: Pass! You can't make a takeout double when your opponents have bid your suits. There are times when the auction gives you no opportunity to show your strength.

Answer 11: Double. That is a penalty double. The opponents are going to have a tough time taking ten tricks. You have at least four tricks in your hand.

Answer 12: 5♡. North's 4NT bid was the Blackwood convention. Your 5♡ response shows that you have two aces. Your partner is looking for slam, and if your heart doesn't pound the first time you bid for slam, you'd better get it checked.

Answer 13: In this hand the solution is pretty natural—bid 2♡. So what's all the fuss? Well, notice something: Your partner might have a diamond suit. There might be a fit in diamonds. He or she also might have four or more hearts. If your partner is going to have a chance to show support in diamonds, or in hearts, he or she will have to do either at the three level (where you need 22 combined points). Therefore, since your bid invites a choice at the three level, it guarantees the combined strength to play at the three level. Since the 1♠ response only promises 6 points, it follows as the day the night that your partner, who knows and trusts that you are thinking, has been assured you have at least 16 points to make this 2♡ bid at this time, since 6 + 16 = 22 and anything less than 16 wouldn't guarantee 22.

Answer 14: 2♢. This hand has the same distribution as the previous hand, but it has minimum strength. Your partner has thus far only guaranteed 6 high-card points. Therefore, for all you know, the partnership may have only 18 combined high-card points. The hand is simply not strong enough to show your hearts on this bid. Now it will be up to your partner. He may pass. He may bid on. He may have a big hand. Who knows? We will leave the completion of this auction to the brooding omnipresence. We do know this: Your partner will continue to describe his hand.

Answer 15: 2♡. You have a big hand. That's a jump shift.

♠
♡
◇
♣

18

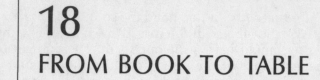
FROM BOOK TO TABLE

Not only do people love the intricacies and satisfactions of bridge, they love the cards themselves. The pasteboards have that smell, and they look so nice. The queen and the jack and the king. The designs are old and close to perfect, and the cards slide so nicely. Some people like the look of the hearts. Some favor the spades or the diamonds. We have never met a club person, but we are sure that there are some out there, and we respect their choice.

Our point is: It is time to get a box of cards and open it and deal out an open hand or two. You are well on your way through this course. You're going to be playing bridge sooner than you think. You are going to have to make the transition from this book to the table.

This book is teaching you. The transition should be without incident—like the magic of a babe on the first night that she sleeps in a bed, not the crib. She just does it. But most parents show her the bed for a few days ahead of time and alert her to the coming excitement. So fondle those cards. We don't want you to think that everything you learned suddenly doesn't apply when those glossy beauties are in your hands.

The transition should, however, be given some thought. When you sit down to play, you have the right to set your pace while you look at your cards. You have the right to insist that you not be hurried. Arrange your cards. Slowly settle yourself down and look at your hand. Count your points precisely. How many spades? "That's not a singleton, it's a doubleton in diamonds." You have come this far in the book, so, yes, these observations are elementary for you, but the road to defender heaven is paved with the sudden fuzzing over of the recently "transitioned" mind.

After the auction, take a moment to switch off any concerns about point count. If you are dummy, get ready to lay down the board. If you are defending, make clear to yourself the number of tricks that you need to set the declarer. If you are declarer, you will soon see the lead, and the dummy. Review in your mind what the others have bid, to translate their bids in order to make a mental note of where certain cards or strength might be. You may ask for a review of the bidding.

Seek the card patterns that you have come to know. They will be there. Let the cards take shape until you can say to yourself, "This is my hand." Do not bid or play until it is as clear in your mind as you think it will get. When you bid and play, don't worry about the fuzzy areas where you are not as certain as you would like to be. They are there for everyone. You know that you must play. You know that you must follow suit. The cards will soon enough show you their logic.

You have a partner. It is a partnership game. Pay attention to your partner.

Watch out for table talk, even legal table talk between hands. Bridge players, those who know more and those who think they know more, love to rattle on between hands about this bid and that, this play and that. Reserve this pleasure for somewhere down the line. These people are guaranteed to confuse you.

There are only two masters when you start to play—
yourself and this book. And, of course, you are responsible
and attentive to your partner. We will allow an exception
for talk between hands with your partner, if it is pointed
and in explanation of something that you or your partner
did. We recommend a thoughtful silence between the hands
for beginning players. Use this chance to take your own
counsel, and do not seek advice or reassurance. Let yourself
learn something. And if absolutely nothing comes to your
mind after a hand, you don't have to say anything.

Then forget about that last hand. Play the next one. Exult
in your victories. Be merciful to yourself in your disasters.
Try to sift through them, to see where it went so wrong.
Don't worry if your lovely 4♡, bid and made, seemed to
accomplish itself without your help. Don't try to make sense
of every step of it. If you make sense of some of it, you are
playing bridge. If you glory at how the game works, if you
use one flash of recognition to make two tricks where lesser
beings would see one, you are on your way.

Many players agree to change partners halfway through
an evening of bridge. When you break for snacks, go over
bidding understandings and signals with your new partner.
Get on the same wavelength. The chat will help to establish
that you are no longer competitors but partners.

And don't be afraid to apply what you are learning from
this book to the situations that are less common. Don't be
afraid to be the first person on your block to make a preemptive bid. If you haven't seen a slam hand ever in your life,
don't be afraid to say, "Four No Trump," when the time
comes. Try to use everything that you have learned. And
trust yourself. Play to see things about the way the cards
work, even things we haven't told you about in this book.

19
PLAYING THE HAND

You have already learned a great deal about playing the hand. The basic idea is to make enough tricks to fulfill your contract. If you can make more ("overtricks"), all well and good.

The following hands demonstrate common problems you will encounter during normal play and ways to solve them. There is no way to present them in a neat outline form. One of the nice things about bridge is that although it appeals to a love of logic, it also takes you away from neat outlines. It is a creative game. Look at these next hands. Take them in. You will see one or more of these playing problems in every hand you play. Feel free to study these hands many times. Don't memorize. Learn from them. You don't "memorize" a friend. You appreciate her, and you keep learning new things about her. Your knowledge of bridge will develop richer and richer layers, as you play more hands.

Solving these problems is one of the joys of the game.

But if you'd like to start off with a hand with no problems, here it is:

> ♠ A
> ♡ A K Q J 10 9
> ◇ A K Q J
> ♣ A K

None of the authors of this book has ever had it or one like it. It calls for the bid of the very best contract, 7NT. A grand slam in one hand. You don't have to think ahead when you play it. It doesn't matter what your partner has. You could not lose a trick if you tried. After the opening lead, you can play them in any order. This is a very rare hand.

Now let's look at hands that are a little more common.

The order of play. The order of play can be as varied as players, hands, and temperament. But it must always have a logic to it. You have already been alerted that you must be careful about transportation. You don't want to come down to the last three rounds with three club winners on the board, yet be stuck in your hand with no clubs and therefore no way to cross over to the board. Here, to make this point vivid, is a picture of that disaster. You are South:

> **North**   ♣ A K Q

> **South**   ♠ 7 2
>   ♡ 9
>
>   Your lead!

Obviously, you should have held a club in your hand, or taken those club tricks earlier, or planned your play so that the tenth trick left you on the board.

In the majority of the contracts played in suits, it is usually a good idea to pull trumps right away.

In certain hands, however, it is best to postpone pulling trumps until you ruff out losers, which means leading losing cards from your hand and trumping them on the board.

Look at this hand. The bidding was:

E	S	W	N
Pass	1♡	Pass	2♡
Pass	3♡	Pass	4♡

North
♠ 9
♡ Q 10 4
◇ Q 9 8 3
♣ K 8 6 4 3

"♠K"

South
♠ A 3
♡ A K 9 8 6 2
◇ 7 5 4
♣ A 9

Declarer has what looks like nine top tricks—six heart winners, two club tricks, and the ♠A. Dummy has a single-ton spade, and declarer has two. Declarer will win the first spade trick. At trick two, the ♠3 should be led and trumped with the ♡4. Then it is time to draw the defenders' trumps and take the rest of the winners.

Playing for the split. Variations of this play come up all the time.

The bidding was:

S	W	N	E
1NT	Pass	3NT	Pass
Pass	Pass		

West led the ♠5. The dummy was spread:

	♠ Q 4
North	♡ A K Q
(dummy)	◇ J 7 4 2
	♣ 9 8 6 2

"♠5"

	♠ A K 7 6
South	♡ 9 6 5 2
(declarer)	◇ A 5 3
	♣ A 7

Actually, although this is a "common" hand, this exact, particular deal of the cards is not any more common than any other deal. Every hand is unique. But these cards do fall into a pattern that you will often see. In this hand, you have to take nine tricks.

Now is the time to think, to plan strategy. Study the cards. Count your winners, your sure bets:

♠A, ♠K, ♠Q, ♡A, ♡K, ♡Q, ◇A, ♣A

That's eight. You need a ninth winner. Do you see any maybes around? Any probables? We see only one. If the defenders' hearts are split 3–3, they will fall on your first three heart tricks, and your fourth heart will be good, for your ninth trick.

Now is the time to work it out in your mind. Be certain that you can return to your hand to enjoy your fourth heart trick after you play dummy's three top hearts. You will need "transportation" back to your hand.

They divide! You are in dummy. Lead the ♠Q, and play the ♠6 from your hand. You are still on the board. Lead ◇2 back to your hand, winning the trick with the ◇A. You have now won six tricks. Now, the ♠A, ♠K, and your fourth heart, all in your hand, are good. That's nine tricks. 3NT bid and made. Nicely done!

We do not want to burden you with a basketfull of statistics. But here are some percentages worth mentioning.

Odds of a "favorable split" in a suit:

You hold	Opponents hold	"Favorable" split	Odds of getting it
9 cards	4 cards	2–2	41%
		3–1	50%
8 cards	5 cards	3–2	68%
		4–1	28%
7 cards	6 cards	3–3	36%
		4–2	48%

Playing for the drop. The idea is similar to playing for the split. But instead of hoping that all of the defenders' cards in the target suit will be drawn, you hope that a specific card or cards are held without sufficient backers, and that it or they will fall on your higher cards.

Look at these North-South spade holdings. You need all of the tricks in the spade suit to make your contract:

North ♠ A K 8 6 5

South ♠ J 9 3 2

Play the ace, followed by the king, hoping that either defender holds the singleton or doubleton queen, and you will pick up the suit for no losers:

You win if:		You lose if:	
Q	10xx	Q10x	x
or		*or*	
Qx	10x	Q10xx	
or			
Q10	xx		

Promoting a winner. Often you have to wait to take your

winners, and you have to prepare the way. In these North-
South holdings . . .

North	◇ 10 7 2
South	◇ K Q J

. . . you are going to have to lose one trick to the ◇A. Play
the ◇K. The ace will cover, and then your queen and jack
will be good. (If the ace does not cover, take your trick and
repeat the process. One way or the other, you will promote
two diamond tricks.)

The finesse. This is one of the most common opportunities to win an extra trick. It comes in several patterns, and
you have seen some of them already. The idea is always
the same—to win a trick, even though the defenders hold a
higher card.

Look at this situation. We are down to three cards. De-
clarer, South, needs all of the tricks to win a club contract.
She is on the board. She knows that the defenders hold the
♠Q and the ♡K and that her ♣J is the only trump left:

North	♠ J
	♡ 9 7
South	♡ A Q
	♣ J

She will try to finesse in the heart suit. The play will
give her a fifty-fifty chance to make an extra trick. She can
see no other way. A fifty-fifty chance is better than nothing.
She will "place" the ♡K in East's hand, and she will play her
cards *as if* that is the case. So she plays the ♡7 from dummy.

Let's see all the cards as declarer makes this play. In this hand, declarer's hopes are realized:

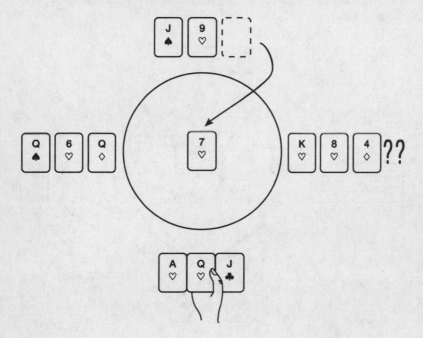

East is stuck.

If East "ducks" and plays the ♡8, declarer will play the ♡Q. That is the same as saying that she will "finesse" the ♡Q.

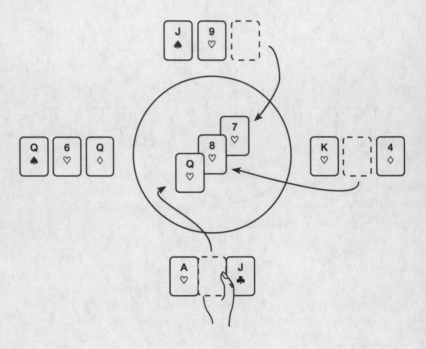

West will play ♡6, under the queen, and declarer will feel wonderful. The ♡A and ♣J are good.

And, suppose that East "goes up" and plays her ♡K. Declarer will have it easy. She will cover with ♡A:

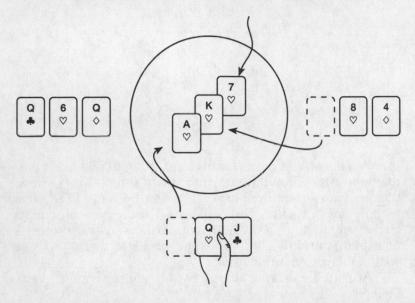

and then, the ♡Q and ♣J are good.

And if it had not worked—if West had shown up with the ♡K—well, nothing ventured, nothing gained. Over the long haul, finesses will work 50 percent of the time. You will be well ahead of the players who never or rarely spot the chance.

Finesses are important, and they are very satisfying when they work. There are many variations, and you will see them. When you plan and make your first finesse, in actual play, your heart will leap with joy. Betcha!

The double finesse: making four spades. You are South, the declarer at 4♠. In this hand, you finesse twice. The key cards are the ♠AQ10. You will finesse the ♠10 *and the ♠* Q.

North

♠ 7 6 5 2
♡ K 9 8 4
◇ 10 3
♣ A Q 2

"◇K"

South
(declarer)

♠ A Q 10 4
♡ A 7
◇ 9 8
♣ K J 8 7 3

You know that the defenders are going to cash their two diamond tricks. You have no club losers and no heart losers. (Assess your losers by focusing on South's hand.) But your trumps are not solid. You will very likely lose one trump trick. The strategy is to hold your trump losers to one, if possible. That will hold your total losers to three, and you will make your contract.

At trick three, after taking two diamond winners, West leads the ♡Q.

The best play is to win the ♡K. Then lead a spade from the board to the ♠10. If West wins the jack, return to the ♣A on the board when you next get the lead. Then lead a spade to the ♠Q, finessing against the missing ♠K.

This play gives you the greatest statistical chance of losing only one spade trick. In fact, your chances are 75 percent. You can see this for yourself. Here are all the possible combinations of the missing honors:

7 6 5 2

(1) K J x   x x   (no play will succeed)

(2) K x   J x x

(3) J x   K x x

(4) x x   K J x

A Q 10 4

Notice that, by finessing the ♠10 first, and then the ♠ Q, you lose two tricks only when West holds both honors—a situation that happens only once in four hands. And, if you do it this way, and if both honors are "on side" (held by East), you will lose no spade.

The finesse: unguarded honor. You can finesse even when the card you are finessing is not sheltered by another, higher card. Look at the holding in the heart suit. You will see this pattern many times:

North   ♡ Q 9

South   ♡ A 4 2

You want to take two tricks in hearts. How would you play it?

Lead from your hand toward the ♡Q, hoping that West holds the ♡K. If he ducks, play the ♡Q. If he plays the ♡K, play dummy's ♡9. The next time that you get to the board, the ♡Q will be a winner. If East holds the ♡K, she will cover your ♡Q, but you will still have made the only play that might have given you two heart tricks.

Making 3NT: choosing among options:

	♠ A Q 5
North	♡ A 9 7
	◇ 9 8 7 5 3
	♣ 6 4

"♣Q"

	♠ 6 3 2
South	♡ K Q J 8
(declarer)	◇ A K 4 2
	♣ A 10

After the attacking lead of the ♣Q, South has only eight sure winners. There are two options available to get your ninth winner. With nine diamonds, if the suit splits 2–2, all the diamond honors will crash, and you will capture five diamond tricks. If the diamond suit does not split favorably, you will have to abandon that suit after your play of the ace and king. Even if diamonds split 3–1, you cannot consider playing another diamond. This play might make sense in some hands, because, after you give up your diamond loser, you would then have cleared the suit and established two more diamond winners.

But in this hand, the defenders, on their opening lead, knocked out your only club stopper, and they are poised to cash at least four club tricks. You cannot give up the lead. You must now take the only chance you have—the spade finesse—to pick up your ninth winner with the ♠ Q.

You *must* try the diamond suit first. If you first tried the spade finesse and it lost, you would have also lost the lead, and the defenders would surely run their club tricks. You would have no chance to come back for the diamond split. If both options fail—well, you should congratulate yourself that you have played it perfectly.

Making six clubs: choosing among options. In this hand, you try one way to make the hand, and, if it doesn't work, you come back and try another way. This is a variation of the theme of the previous hand.

The bidding:

S	W	N	E
1♣	Pass	3♣	Pass
4NT	Pass	5◇	Pass
6♣	Pass	Pass	Pass
Pass			

What happened? North responded to South's opening 1♣ bid with a jump raise. South used Blackwood to ask for aces.

Question: North's 5◇ bid said that she had . . . ?

Answer: One ace. 5♣ would have meant 0 or 4. When you are using Blackwood or Gerber, do not hesitate to count off the code carefully in your head.

Obviously, South found out what she wanted to know. She bid slam.

The opening lead was the ♡A. Dummy was spread. Here are the North-South hands:

	♠ A Q 7
	♡ 10 6
North	◇ 9 6
	♣ K Q 10 9 7 3
"♡A"	
	♠ K 6 5 3
South	♡ K Q
(declarer)	◇ A Q 8
	♣ A J 4 2

West won the first trick and continued the heart suit. Declarer won the trick and then pulled trump in two rounds. She has to take all of the rest of the tricks. It looks as if she is going to have to take the diamond finesse to make her slam.

Before she does, she can try another way to make her twelfth trick without any risk. She has three spade winners. She can play for a fourth spade winner if the defenders' spades split 3–3. The diamond finesse will be unnecessary.

If spades split 4–2, declarer can still come back and try the finesse of the ◇Q, with a fifty-fifty chance of success. Notice that she must take the spades option first. If she tries the diamond finesse first and loses the ◇Q to the ◇K, the hand will be over, and she will be down one, too late to play for the split in spades.

Question: If declarer loses the diamond finesse, that would mean that, in this hand, the ◇K turned up in which defender's hand?

Answer: West.

Making 4♠: *crossruff.* This is one of the most delightful ways to make a suit contract. North and South have the contract at 4♠:

<table>
<tr><td></td><td>♠ A Q 10 2</td></tr>
<tr><td>**North**</td><td>♡ A 7 6 5</td></tr>
<tr><td></td><td>◇ 2</td></tr>
<tr><td></td><td>♣ K 10 6 2</td></tr>
</table>

"◇Q"

<table>
<tr><td></td><td>♠ K J 9 7</td></tr>
<tr><td>**South**</td><td>♡ 4 3 2</td></tr>
<tr><td>**(declarer)**</td><td>◇ A 7 5 4 3</td></tr>
<tr><td></td><td>♣ A</td></tr>
</table>

You have eight top winners, not enough for your contract. But with a "crossruff" you can take twelve tricks. You never pull trump, but instead merrily ruff cards in both hands.

Trick (1) ◇A
     (2) ◇3, ruffed in dummy with ♠2
     (3) cash ♡A
     (4) return to hand with ♣A
     (5) ◇4, ruffed with ♠10
     (6) ♣K, discarding ♡2
     (7) ♣6, ruffed with ♠7
     (8) ◇5, ruffed with ♠Q
     (9) ♣10, ruffed with ♠9
    (10) ◇7, ruffed with ♠A

With three tricks to go, you are now left with the two highest trump and a losing heart, making twelve tricks.

When you plan to crossruff, you must cash your high-card winners as soon as you can. Remember that as the tricks are played, the defenders may have a chance to discard all of their cards in a suit, giving them the chance to ruff one of your high card winners later in the play.

This hand is a dramatic demonstration of how to produce tricks by using trumps individually.

You made twelve tricks, and, if you had bid it, you would have scored a slam. You can be excused for not bidding to 6♠ with this hand. The point count in both hands was not there, and you would have had to have X-ray eyes to see this beautiful playing fit. As we have said, no bidding system is perfect.

Making 6♡: to finesse, or not to finesse. Here is a decision you will face again and again:

S	W	N	E
1NT	Pass	2♣ (Stayman)	Pass
2♡	Pass	4♣ (Gerber)	Pass
4♠ (2 aces)	Pass	6♡	Pass
Pass	Pass		

North

♠ K Q 2
♡ A K 7 6
◇ 8
♣ K Q 7 5 4

"◇A"

♠ A J 9
♡ J 10 9 3
◇ K Q J 2
♣ A 8

South
(declarer)

West cashed his ◇A. He then led ♠4.

You must take all the rest. The problem is to limit your losers in the trump suit to zero. You must pick up the suit.

Your decision is: Should you play ♡A followed by ♡K, in the hope that the missing ♡Q will drop? . . . or . . .

Should you lead from your hand with ♡J to take the finesse, hoping that West holds the ♡Q?

The answer, in this hand, is . . . take the finesse.

If you are missing the queen, and holding the AKJ10, with fewer than nine cards, the finesse is the correct percentage play. (With eight cards, you have a slightly better than 27 percent chance of finding the queen as a singleton, or backed by only one card. With nine cards, the queen will drop in a little better than 50 percent of all hands.)

> So: missing the queen, and holding AKJ10 with nine cards in a suit, don't finesse. Play for the drop;
>
> with eight or fewer cards, finesse.

Our advice is expressed in the bridge axiom for this holding: "Eight ever, nine never."

Here is the hand again:

North

♠ K Q 2
♡ A K 7 6
◇ 8
♣ K Q 7 5 4

"◇A"

South
(declarer)

♠ A J 9
♡ J 10 9 3
◇ K Q J 2
♣ A 8

After you win the spade at trick two, your best approach is first to play the ♡A, in case the ♡Q does happen to be a singleton. When the ♡Q doesn't drop, return to your hand and play the ♡J, letting it ride. If that wins, repeat the finesse, leading ♡10.

Making 3NT. You must always be mindful of the bidding when you play. In this hand, the bidding tells you the percentage play.

Absorb the bidding. Get a solid sense of the hands.

S	W	N	E
1♣	1◇	1♠	Pass
1NT	Pass	3NT	Pass
Pass	Pass		

West leads the ◇J. Dummy is spread. Here are the North-South hands:

North

♠ A J 9 6
♡ A Q 8
◇ 7 4
♣ Q 9 8 2

"◇J"

South
(declarer)

♠ Q 10 2
♡ K 6 3 2
◇ K 6
♣ A J 10 7

West leads his suit, knocking out your only diamond stopper. If the defenders get the lead again, they will cash enough diamond tricks to defeat the contract. (When West overcalled, he had to have had at least five diamonds.)

You have two ways to make your ninth trick—to finesse in either clubs or spades. The bidding tells you that it is likely that West has the majority of the missing high cards. Therefore, although there is no guarantee, it makes sense to take the spade finesse, since East is unlikely to have the missing honors.

Notice that in this hand you do not have the luxury of trying the club finesse and then the spade finesse. Whichever finesse you try, if you lose, you are going down in a flurry of diamonds.

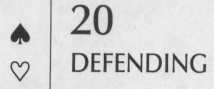

20
DEFENDING

The purpose of defending is to set the contract. It begins in the bidding. A preemptive bid is a defensive bid, designed to make it difficult for your opponents to communicate except by bids at high levels. A "business" or "penalty" double is a defensive bid. An overcall is often used to call for a lead (another reason why you need a good suit to overcall). Another opportunity for defensive bidding is a hand in which you will lose fewer points if you make a sacrifice bid than your opponents would score if you let them play the hand. And all bids give defensive information; they reveal information about where the cards may lie.

In the play of the cards, it is vital to remember that the defense gets first thrust with the opening lead. That is a crucial opportunity for the partnership to take tricks and to establish later tricks. At the moment of the opening lead, the defenders are in control. The goals of the opening leader follow on page 205.

• Attack weaknesses. For example, if the opponents have bid three suits, lead the fourth;

• Build up your own suits before they are trumped. You do this either by taking a trick or playing a card that will promote a winner for yourself or your partner later in the hand.

There is no one hard-and-fast rule that will cover all situations. You always consider your partner's hand. If your partner has bid a suit, lead that suit. That is called "leading to partner's strength." Always lead your partner's bid suit unless you have a play that is clearly better.

If you are in doubt, it is safe to lead through dummy's strength. That is, it is usually safe to lead the suit that dummy bid.

Here are some additional rules of thumb to throw into the mix. If you don't have a lot of power, attack—try to find partner's strength. It might be worth a risky lead.

If you have a lot of power, and you are defending, partner can't have much. Don't lead a suit that has an honor in it. Make a conservative lead and hope that your tricks will come to you.

Consider leading a singleton if the opponents have not bid the suit. Your partner might win the trick and lead back the suit for you to trump.

If you hold an unsupported ace, do not lead that suit unless you have a very good reason.

Against a No-Trump contract, with no better lead, lead fourth best from your longest and strongest suit, provided the opponents have not bid it.

Once you have decided on the suit to lead, which card should you lead?

If you hold "touching honors," or three cards in "sequence," lead the highest. This assures your partner that you hold the next highest card:

       AKx   lead A
       KQ   lead K
       QJxx   lead Q

These are sequences:

QJ10	lead Q
J109x	lead J
1098xx	lead 10

Also lead the highest card from a "broken sequence":

QJ9	lead Q
J108x	lead J
1097	lead 10

If you hold three or four cards that are not in sequence, lead low:

K97	lead 7
Q83	lead 3
Q1063	lead 3

If you hold five cards that are not in sequence, lead fourth best:

Q10632	lead 3

If you hold two cards in a suit, lead the higher card:

94	lead 9
J8	lead J

If you are leading your partner's suit, the rules are the same, except when you have supported the suit in the bidding and *you do not have an honor*, lead high with any holding:

1074	lead 10
K95	lead 5 (as always)

All of the card strategies, such as finessing, and even concerns about transportation to your partner's hand, are exactly the same as they would be if you were playing the hand. The cards are the cards and they work the same way.

The only difference is that you cannot see each other's hands. And, you do not have to take as many tricks as the opponents. You will try to imagine what your partner holds, and you will be aided by her bids. You may also be aided by card signals and by the fall of the cards as the play continues.

During the play, a general rule is: If your opponent is on lead, and you are in second seat, play low. If partner leads, play high.

Defending against 4♠: promoting a trump trick for the defense.

You are East. The bidding was:

N	E	S	W
1♣	Pass	1♠	Pass
2♣	Pass	3♠	Pass
4♠			

North opened 1♣. South responded 1♠ and then jumped to show a long suit and an opening bid. North raised to game.

Here are all of the hands:

	North (dummy)	
	♠ 9 8	
	♡ 9 8 2	
	◇ A K 9	
	♣ A K 9 5 4	

West		East
♠ J 6 2		♠ 10 5
♡ K Q J		♡ A 10 4 3
◇ Q 8 5 2		◇ 10 7 6 3
♣ J 8 7		♣ 10 6 2

	South (declarer)	
	♠ A K Q 7 4 3	
	♡ 7 6 5	
	◇ J 4	
	♣ Q 3	

East-West needed four tricks to set the contract.

West led his good hearts, first the ♡K and then the ♡Q. On the third trick, he led the ♡J.

Question: If you were East. What would you, East, play? Study this one. This is for a gold star. You have an advantage—we're letting you see all of the cards.

Answer: Overtake your partner's good ♡J with your ♡A! With no diamond or club trick possible, the only play is to promote a trump in West's hand. As Mrs. Culbertson said, "Play 'em the way they have to lie."

Question: Now what do you play?
Answer: The thirteenth heart!

This is the way it looks as East (you) leads the ♡10 at the fourth trick:

```
                        ♠ 9 8
                        ♡
                        ◇ A K 9
                        ♣ A K 9 5 4

    ♠ J 6 2                                    ♠ 10 5
    ♡                          "H10"           ♡ *
    ◇ Q 8 5 2                                  ◇ 10 7 6 3
    ♣ J 8 7                                    ♣ 10 6 2

                        ♠ A K Q 7 4 3
                        ♡
                        ◇ J 4
                        ♣ Q 3
```

There is nothing that declarer can do. East has successfully promoted a trump trick in her partner's hand, before
declarer has had a chance to draw trumps:
• If declarer ruffs with a low trump, West will overruff
with the ♠J.
• If declarer discards, in order to trump in dummy, West
will trump with his ♠J, which will beat any trump in
dummy.
• If declarer trumps high with ♠AK or Q, West will
discard. Now his ♠J, with two backers, cannot be "drawn,"
because declarer will be left with only two remaining high
trump. Eventually, the ♠J must become a winner.
That was a very elegant play, East.
Signals. Signals are not always possible, because you
must use the actual cards that you play to give the signal.
For example, if you wanted your partner to lead a suit, you
might get your message across by discarding an ace, but you
would also be throwing away a trick. Still, there are many
occasions when you can signal and still hold on to the cards
you want.
When you are following suit, a high card signals to your
partner that you want the suit continued, and a low card
signals the opposite. Similarly, when you have your first opportunity to discard, a high card in the suit you are discarding shows you would like that suit to be led. If you
cannot spare a high card in the suit you want, discard a low
card in the suit you do not want. Your partner should be
able to figure out what you *do* want.
Signaling with a "high card" doesn't mean wasting an
honor. If you hold ♠AQ92, you would signal with the ♠9.
Hopefully, your partner would understand.
Signals have to be read in context. You should be alert
to each other for signals. Sometimes it's easy to pick up your
partner's signal. Suppose your partner plays ♠8. If you saw
♠KJx in dummy, and you held ♠Q109, your partner's ♠8
would be the highest card your partner could have in spades
besides the ace.
Sometimes a signal is made clear in two rounds of the
suit. "High-low" signals an even number of cards in the suit,
usually two. Look at the situations on page 210.

The contract is 4♡. South is declarer. You are East. You hold:

♠ 6 2
♡ J 4 3
◇ A 10 8 5 4
♣ 8 7 4

Your partner leads ♠A. At your turn, play ♠6. West has led from touching honors. He can play ♠K on the next round and your ♠2 will complete your signal of your doubleton in spades. He can play spades on the third round for you to trump. It looks as though declarer is going down.

Question: You are West, defending with your partner against 4♠. The bidding was:

S	W	N	E
1♠	Pass	2♠	Pass
4♠	Pass	Pass	Pass

It is trick five. South leads the ♠K:

North

♠ 6 4
♡ J 5 9
◇ A K
♣ J 3

West

♠
♡ A Q 3 2
◇ 7 6 5
♣ 6 4

"♠ K"   (South's lead)

What card would you play? Take your time.
Answer: ♣4.

Declarer is pulling the last trump, which is in East's
hand. You are out of trumps and can discard. You should
discard the ♣4. This low card should deny any interest in
the club suit. It is a discouraging signal that announces,
"Don't play clubs." If East gets in, she should switch to hearts
as the only source of possible tricks for the defense. (Look
at dummy's diamonds.) When East leads a heart, if declarer
ducks, you win with the ♡Q. If declarer plays ♡K, you cover
with the ♡A, and then your ♡Q is good.

If you had held a high heart that you could afford to
discard, you would have discarded that card as an encouraging signal. That would have been a more obvious way of
sending the same message.

21
THE GODS OF BRIDGE

This night, you pair off with Bones, and Sally and Drilla go off to who-knows-where to discuss things.

"We want to know what system you're playing," says Drilla, as she emerges from their secret place, her nails newly polished bright red. Drilla is really ready.

"Yeah," says Sally. They are together in this.

"No problem," you say. "We have to tell you that. Tell 'em, Bones."

"We're playing five-card majors, Stayman, Gerber, and Blackwood, of course."

"Of course," says Drilla.

"And," Bones goes on, "preemptive bids with seven or more cards in the suit and five to nine high-card points."

"Bones," you say, "that's right! This will be a good night."

"We'll see," says Drilla. Sally looks very determined.

"Well, what are you guys playing?" Bones asks.

"Same thing," says Sally. "Deal 'em."

First hand. You are South. You are declarer.

You are on the board. It is the twelfth trick. You need two tricks to make the contract. Here are the cards. Drilla is East:

What would you play? ♠6. Sure. Going for the finesse. You don't really have much choice.

You play ♠6. Drilla plays ♠9. You hope that she has the king, and that she has ducked.

So, you are in your hand. In your mind, you play ♠Q. But, in fact, to your amazement, you look down and see that you put ♠A on the table! Oh my! Oh no! Now Drilla's ♠K is good.

What can you do? Take it back? Can you say, "Whoops, let me take that back. I meant to play the ♠Q. Oh, really. Oh, surely you can see that. I was going for the finesse"?

Zot! It's the Gods of Bridge. "A Card Laid Is a Card Played," they resonate. No excuses. No ifs, ands, or maybes. No take-backs.

"Oh, but . . . Oh, ple-e-ease."

Not a chance.

They are strict, these gods. And Drilla and Sally are right behind them. "A Card Laid Is a Card Played," they croon.

It is absolutely the best rule. Otherwise, the hands get sloppy. The rule makes for the best game. Play by it. Don't accidentally play the wrong card. No whining when you do. The only sounds during a hand of bridge should be the bids, and the voice of the declarer calling for cards to be played from dummy.

Well. Folks do sometimes mutter, "I guess it's my lead" and the like, which is considered acceptable. It is never polite to tell someone, "It's your lead." "Whose lead is it?" said gently, after a very long pause, is considered polite in cities beginning with the letter K.

22
COMPLETE SCORING

If you bid and make a game contract, you have a "game on."

If you bid and make a contract that is less than game, for example, 2♣, you have a "part score," often called a "partial."

If you have a part score, and you make another part score, you will have a game if the your scores add up to 100 or more.

Points for "overtricks" (tricks that you take in excess of your bid), defensive points for "undertricks," and slam bonuses do not help you to reach "game," but they will count in the final tally.

Once one partnership scores a game, the other team's "partial" is "wiped off." That is, the points will not count toward reaching the next game, but they will count in the final tally.

If you have scored one game, you are "vulnerable." You will score more points if you make your next contract, and you will be penalized more points if you fail to make your next contract.

If the other team makes the next game, both teams are "vulnerable."

When a team wins two games, that completes the "rubber" and they get a bonus.

Your score pad for each rubber should look like this:

WE   **THEY**

Notice the line across the score pad. All of the tricks that you make and you have bid are scored "below the line." For example, if you bid and make 3♡, all of those points will be written in, literally, below the line. If you bid 3♡ and make four, the points for three tricks will be scored below the line, and the points for your "overtrick" will be scored "above the line." If the contract is doubled, the doubled value is scored below the line. That means that if you make your doubled 2♡ bid, you have been "doubled into game."

Points for "overtricks," defensive points for "undertricks," and bonuses for slam are scored "above the line."

When the rubber is completed, add up all of the points below and above the line. The winner is the team with the most points.

In the scoring system, the emphasis is on game and on rubber.

Even so, you can score a lot of points and never make a game: If your opponents go down, doubled and vulnerable, several hands in a row, you will not be scoring points "below the line," but you will be scoring a lot of points. If you score enough defensive points, you could actually win a rubber without making any games.

If players keep "going down," it can take several hands before one team scores two games.

The big scores come from games, slams, and setting your opponents many "undertricks." For example, the score for setting your opponents five down, doubled and vulnerable (a disaster!) is 1,400 points.

Question: What does "setting your opponent five tricks, doubled and vulnerable" mean?

Answer: It means that the opponents bid to take five more tricks than they were able to take. In other words, they have five "undertricks." An example would be if they bid 5♣ and took only six tricks, instead of eleven.

"Doubled" means that, after the five bid, one of the defenders upped the ante.

"Vulnerable" means that these poor souls already had a "game on."

In such a hand, once the last trick is gathered in, usually, if not always, after a polite pause, one of the defenders says sweetly, "Down five, doubled and vulnerable." You will detect a little note of music in his or her voice.

This is the most catastrophic situation in bridge. If your opponents are dealt powerful cards and they bid and make a grand slam, you can not fault yourself. But to go down five, or four, or three, or even two, in your own contract! What a mixup you had with your partner in the bidding! What a horror of loss of control as you watch your opponents scoop up the tricks and try to keep themselves from snickering. It is time that we faced up to it. There can be grim moments in this game. But, there is always the next hand.

Question: Look at this score card:

N-S	E-W
60	100

Who is vulnerable?
Answer: East-West. They have 100 points below the line and have made game.

Question: How many hands have been played?
Answer: Two. We can see that North-South made a partial score. East-West bid to game in one hand, and they made it.

Question:

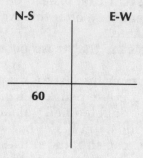

North-South, as you can see, have a "partial" of 60 points. If they want to make a game in the next hand, what contract or contracts should they be looking for?
Answer: 1NT or anything higher. 1NT (as well as 2♣ or 2◇) will give them 40 points, which, combined with the 60 they already have, make game. If they make overtricks, all of them will be scored, just as valuably, above the line.

Moral: Don't bid a game contract if all you need is a partial score. Stop when you reach the contract that will give you the partial score, unless you think you might have a slam.

You now have the essentials of scoring. For specifics, see the scoring table on page 219. Get the sense of it. Don't try to memorize it. Consult it for strategic purposes, and use it to tally the score after you play each hand.

SCORING TABLE

Trick Value (Only if you make the hand!):

♣	20
◇	20
♡	30
♠	30
NT	40 first trick
	30 each additional trick

Doubled: multiply score by 2
Redoubled: multiply score by 4

Overtrick Value:	Vulnerable	Not Vulnerable
undoubled	Trick Value	
doubled	100	200
redoubled	200	400
bonus for making doubled contract	50	50
bonus for making redoubled contract	100	100
(above the line)		

Undertrick Value:	Not Vunerable		Vulnerable	
Down	Undoubled	Doubled	Undoubled	Doubled
1	50	100	100	200
2	100	300	200	500
3	150	500	300	800
4	200	800	400	1100
5	250	1100	500	1400
Additional, per trick	50	300	100	300

If redoubled, multiply score by 2

Bonuses for rubber and slam:

Rubber, if other team has no game	700
Rubber, if other team has a game on	500

	Not Vulnerable	Vulnerable
Small slam	500	750
Grand slam	1000	1500

Extra bonuses:

Honors (if held in one hand):

Four "honors" (AKQJ) in trump suit, even if down	100
Five "honors" (AKQJ10) in trump suit, even if down	150
Four aces at No Trump, even if down	150

Look at how those numbers begin to leap as undertricks go up, as contracts are doubled, and as teams are vulnerable.

Moral: Every moral you can think of. Bid with care. Don't redouble heedlessly. For that matter, don't double heedlessly. Be even more alert when you or they are vulnerable.

Question: The score card is blank. East-West bid 3♣ and are doubled. They make it. What score would you write, and where?

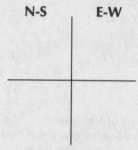

N-S   E-W

Answer: Score 120 points below the line. The 20 points for each trick, boosted to 40 (the doubled value of tricks), is scored below the line. They were "doubled into game." They now have a game on! And they also score the 50-point bonus above the line for making a doubled contract—"50 points for the insult."

Here's a quick scoring quiz:

Question	Answer
What is "game"?	100 points
How many scoring points is one trick in clubs?	20 points
What is another word for having a game on?	vulnerable
What is 4♠, made and doubled?	240 points plus 50

What is 4♠, made, doubled, and redoubled?   480 points plus 100

What is the bonus for a small slam, not vulnerable?   500 points

What is the bonus for a grand slam, vulnerable?   1,500 points

What is the score for winning the rubber?   depends if the other side has a game on

What is the score for an overtrick in diamonds?   20 points

Would it be more if doubled?   yes

What is the score for 4♠, down one, doubled and vulnerable?   200 points

Once one team has made game, draw a line underneath the scoring and set up your pad to score the second game. For example, if N-S bid and made four spades, and then E-W bid and made two diamonds, the score pad would look like this:

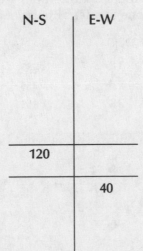

N-S	E-W
120	
	40

23
PUTTING IT ALL TOGETHER

Here are a few closing exercises to help you to see bidding, playing, and scoring as a seamless whole.

You are South. You are vulnerable. In the previous hand you bid and made one spade. This has been the bidding:

W	N	E	S
Pass	1♣	Pass	1♡
Pass	1♠	Pass	2♡
Pass	3♡	Pass	?

This is your hand:

♠ 4 3
♡ K J 9 7 6 4
◇ K 3 2
♣ 9 6

Question: What should you bid?

Answer: Pass. You already have 30 points for making
1♠. 3♡ will now give you 90 points and game.

West leads the ♣5. Here are the cards that you can see:

North

♠ A J 7 6
♡ Q 8 2
◇ 10 9
♣ A K 10 3

"♣5"

South
(declarer)

♠ 4 3
♡ K J 9 7 6 4
◇ K 3 2
♣ 9 6

Question: How would you play the hand? Think out
your strategy. It wouldn't hurt to study the hands and then
write down your strategy clearly, so that you will be certain
whether or not you agree with us. Start with your sure
winners.

Answer: You have five hearts, one spade, and two clubs
off the top. That's eight. The bid is 3♡. You need nine. At
trick two, play a diamond toward the ◇K in your hand. If
the ◇A is on side, the ◇K will be the ninth trick. If it loses,
play another diamond when you next get the lead. Ruff your
third diamond in dummy before pulling trumps.

Here are all four hands:

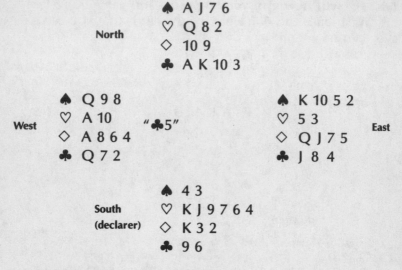

North
♠ A J 7 6
♡ Q 8 2
◇ 10 9
♣ A K 10 3

West
♠ Q 9 8
♡ A 10
◇ A 8 6 4
♣ Q 7 2

"♣5"

East
♠ K 10 5 2
♡ 5 3
◇ Q J 7 5
♣ J 8 4

South
(declarer)
♠ 4 3
♡ K J 9 7 6 4
◇ K 3 2
♣ 9 6

It will work. (Even if the ◇K had won, you would have
completed the strategy of playing another diamond and
trumping it in dummy before pulling trumps—for an overtrick.)

Question: You are West. North-South are vulnerable.
The bidding was:

S	W	N	E
1♠	Dble	2♠	Pass
3♠	Pass	4♠	Pass
Pass	?		

These are your cards. What would you bid now, on the
third round of bidding?

♠ K 7
♡ K Q 10 5
◇ 10 8 2
♣ A K 9 4

Answer: Double. That is a very good bid. That is a "business double." (Your first double was a takeout double. Your partner was not forced to respond because North interposed his 2♠ bid.) Now you really mean it. You don't think that they can take ten tricks. You look at your hand and see one spade trick, one or two heart tricks, and two definite club tricks—possibly five defensive tricks. Even if one of them doesn't materialize, the contract will still be down. North and South are vulnerable. It is definitely time to venture a business double.

Question: Everyone now passes. It's your lead. What would you lead?
Answer: ♣A. It's a trick, and you will get to see the dummy.

The dummy is spread:

North	♠ Q 4 2
(dummy)	♡ A J 4
	◇ Q 7 3
	♣ 10 8 6 5

	♠ K 7	
West	♡ K Q 10 5	
(you)	◇ 10 8 2	"♣A"
	♣ * K 9 4	

Watch the cards. Watch your partner's cards.

	W	N (dummy)	E	S
Trick 1	♣A	♣5	♣7	♣3
Trick 2	♣K	♣6	♣2	♣J

Question: What would you lead now?
Answer: A club. Your partner, East, "echoed"—"high-low." This signal means an even number of cards, usually two. Continue with a club for your partner to ruff.

Here are all of the hands:

North
- ♠ Q 4 2
- ♡ A J 4
- ◇ Q 7 3
- ♣ 10 8 6 5

West (you)
- ♠ K 7
- ♡ K Q 10 5
- ◇ 10 8 2
- ♣ A K 9 4

East (your partner)
- ♠ 8 6
- ♡ 8 7 6 3 2
- ◇ 9 6 5 4
- ♣ 7 2

South (declarer)
- ♠ A J 10 9 5 3
- ♡ 9
- ◇ A K J
- ♣ Q J 3

With three tricks in, you will still get your ♠K. (One of the prospects of your defense was the possibility of a heart trick, which did not materialize. Declarer had only one heart in his hand and hence no loser.) Notice that if you hadn't played the third club back, declarer would have taken control with any other lead, drawn trumps, and would have made his contract.

Declarer would have made four spades, doubled and vulnerable, for a score of 240 plus 50 "for the insult" plus 500 for game and rubber—790 points.

Instead, North-South are down one, doubled and vulnerable, for minus 200. That's a swing of 990 points, all for trusting your partner's signal.

Question: You are South, vulnerable, and you are dealt this hand:

♠ K 6 4
♡ 5
◇ A Q J 10 7
♣ A 9 5 3

The bidding has been:

E	S	W	N
	1◇	Pass	1♡
Pass	2♣	Pass	3♡
Pass	?		

What would you bid?

Answer: 3NT. Partner's first response showed at least four hearts, and his jump to 3♡ showed at least five hearts and a full opening bid. The partnership has game-level points and must bid a game. With no fit in any suit, and having the unbid suit stopped, the natural bid is 3NT.

After the 3NT bid, everyone passes. West leads the ♠3. The dummy is spread:

North
♠ A 8
♡ A J 8 6 2
◇ K 5 2
♣ 10 7 2

"♠3"

South
(declarer)
♠ K 6 4
♡ 5
◇ A Q J 10 7
♣ A 9 5 3

It looks as if you're in the right contract.

Question: How would you play the hand?

Answer: Your partnership has nine top tricks—two spades, one heart, five diamonds, one club. Take them from the top!

Here are all of the cards:

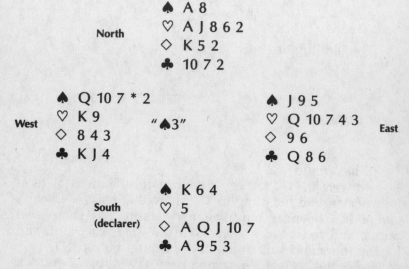

             ♠ A 8

North   ♡ A J 8 6 2

             ◇ K 5 2

             ♣ 10 7 2

♠ Q 10 7 * 2   ♠ J 9 5

♡ K 9   "♠3"   ♡ Q 10 7 4 3

West ◇ 8 4 3   ◇ 9 6 East

♣ K J 4   ♣ Q 8 6

            ♠ K 6 4

South   ♡ 5

(declarer) ◇ A Q J 10 7

            ♣ A 9 5 3

That's 3NT, vulnerable, for 100 points below the line. It is also game, and thus another 500 points for rubber. That's a total of 600 points. Not a bad hand.

And that is the last hand in this book.

You have the foundation on which to build beautiful bridge and to play the game well.

The hands have grown more challenging, and we haven't always explained every single step. But you have struggled to follow, and you have succeeded. The core of this great game is in you now. Deal 'em!

24

HEADING INTO DESTINY

It is a balmy spring night, the kind of night that stirs the soul to certain knowledge of diamond destiny. You have showered and powdered, and although the night is quiet you know that this will not be just any night.

Question: Does the phone ring?
Answer: Of course.

It is Lothar. He wants to know—ha-ha—if you want to sit in on this great new game, since Quilla, their usual robot fourth, is going to the Kabuki.

It is by the most amazing coincidence that your brand-new, just-opened pack of fifty-two is humming on the table. You reach for it. You cozy it inside your thumb and fingers, deep. You snug the first digits of your fingers around the far edge of the pack—force the edge into the creases of your fingers. You squeeze the shiny celluloids. The edges won't cut you, but it's close.

A part of you—tightens. But a part of you—is ready! A smile of perfect cowboy confidence snakes across your mouth. The poor sucker doesn't know that you've read *Building Bridge.*

"Okay, Lothar."

Glossary

Above the Line (See Below the Line.)

Auction The bidding of all four players for the contract.

Below the Line All scores that count toward game are entered below the horizontal line on the score sheet. All additional scores (including points by the defense, bonuses for slam and rubber, honors, and overtricks) are scored above the horizontal line.

Blackwood A bidding convention ("4 No Trump") that asks your partner how many aces he holds.

Contract The outcome of the auction—the goal of the declarer, which the defense will attempt to defeat.

Convention An artificial bid that, by agreement, has a specific meaning for your partner (see Blackwood, Gerber, and Stayman).

Cover To play a higher card than your right-hand opponent has just played.

Crossruff The use of trumps separately whereby losers are ruffed by both dummy and declarer (see Ruff).

Declarer The person who first named the contract suit; he or she "plays" the hand.

Defenders, Defend The opponents of the declarer, whose object is to defeat the contract.

Distribution The way the thirteen cards are divided among the suits in any given hand; the "shape" of your hand.

Double A bid that increases the scoring (see Takeout Double).

Doubleton A holding of two cards in a suit.

Dummy The declarer's partner. After the opening lead, his or her hand is exposed on the table. During the play, "on the board" means that the next card is to be played from the dummy.

Duplicate Bridge A form of bridge in which there is more than one table and the same hand is played at each table.

Echo A signal by the defense, in which a higher card is played on the first round of the suit, then followed by a lower card.

Favorable Split (See Split.)

Finesse The play of a card in the hope that its position will win a trick, even though a higher card is outstanding. This works when the hand with the higher card must play before the card that you hope to win with.

Fit Two hands that play well together. The term is used particularly in reference to the trump suit.

Forcing Bid A bid that requires your partner to make a bid other than "pass."

Game Achieving 100 points below the line. The first team to win two games wins the rubber.

Gerber A bidding convention ("4 clubs") that asks your partner how many aces he or she holds. This convention is used after an opening bid of No Trump.

Grand Slam Bidding and making all thirteen tricks.

High-Low (See Echo.)

Honor A high card.

Jump Bid A bid that skips a level in a suit you previously bid.

Jump Raise A bid that skips a level in a suit your partner previously bid.

Jump Shift A bid that changes suit at a higher level than necessary.

Kibitzing Watching people play bridge.

Lefty The person who sits on your left.

Major Suits Hearts and spades.

Minor Suits Clubs and diamonds.

No Trump A bid or contract designating that there will be no trump suit.

Non-vulnerable A scoring term designating that a team (or teams) has not yet scored a game (see Vulnerable).

On the Board (See Dummy.)

Open the Bidding After the cards are dealt, to make the first bid other than a "pass."

Opening Lead After the bidding is concluded, the first card played. The lead is made by declarer's left-hand opponent.

Overcall To bid over your opponent's opening bid.

Overtrick, Overtricks A trick or tricks in excess of the number of tricks required by the contract.

Part Score, Partial A contract made that is less than game.

Point Count A system for evaluating the strength of a hand, based on the valuation of its honor cards and the distribution.

Preempt   A defensive bid indicating a long suit, with limited strength.

Rebid   To make any second or further bid.

Redouble   A bid made over a "double" that further increases the scoring (see Double). It is sometimes used to describe strength.

Response   A bid made after your partner has opened.

Righty   The person who sits on your right.

Rubber   (See Game.)

Ruff   To win a trick by using trump, when the hand is void in the suit that was led.

Shape   (See Distribution.)

Signal   Card play by which defenders indicate information about their hands.

Singleton   A holding of one card in a suit.

Slam   (See Small Slam and Grand Slam.)

Small Slam   Bidding and making twelve tricks.

Split   The distribution of the cards in the defenders' hands in any given suit. A "favorable split" is one in which the cards are divided evenly in the defenders' hands, or, if they hold an odd number of cards, as evenly as possible.

Stayman   A bidding convention ("two clubs") used after an opening No-Trump bid. It is used to uncover major-suit fits.

Stopper   A high card or cards limiting the number of tricks the opponents can win in any given suit.

Takeout Double   A bid made after the opponents have opened the bidding. It requests your partner to bid an unbid suit.

Trick   Four cards played one after the other. There are thirteen tricks in every bridge hand.

Trump   The suit designated as the master or "power" suit, also used as a synonym for "ruff" (see Ruff).

Undertrick, Undertricks   A trick or tricks fewer than the number required by the contract.

Void   The absence of cards in a given suit. Also, once you have played all of your cards in a suit, you are now "void."

Vulnerable   A scoring term designating that a team (or teams) has scored a game (see Non-vulnerable).

Index

ARNOLD FISHER is a professional bridge player. He is an American Life Master and a World Master, with more than 9,000 master points. He is the most sought-after bridge teacher on the East Coast.

BO SCHAMBELAN is a writer, lawyer, and teacher. He has successfully used the techniques of this book to teach law to college students. He is a lover of bridge. He was a beginner until he worked with Arnold Fisher on this book. Now he considers himself a solid beginner.

RICHARD LEDERER is a teacher and a writer of best-selling language books. Working with Bo Schambelan and Arnold Fisher, he has come to appreciate, even more, the beauty of bridge language.